TIGER STYLE!

BY MIKE LEW

★

★

DRAMATISTS
PLAY SERVICE
INC.

The world premiere of TIGER STYLE! was produced by the Alliance Theatre (Susan V. Booth, Artistic Director), Atlanta, Georgia, in September 2015. It was directed by Moritz von Stuelpnagel, the scenic design was by Wilson Chin, the costume design was by Amy Clark, the sound design was by Palmer Hefferan, the projection design was by Alex Koch, and the lighting design was by Ken Yunker. The cast was as follows:

ALBERT CHEN .... Jon Norman Schneider
JENNIFER CHEN .... Ruibo Qian
RUSS THE BUS/REGGIE/
CUSTOMS GUY .... Bobby Labartino
TZI CHUAN/MELVIN/DAD/
GENERAL TSO .... Francis Jue
THERAPIST/MOM/COUSIN CHEN/
MATCHMAKER .... Emily Kuroda

TIGER STYLE! was developed during a residency at the Eugene O'Neill Theater Center's (Preston Whiteway, Executive Director; Wendy C. Goldberg, Artistic Director) National Playwrights Conference in 2014.

CHARACTERS

ALBERT CHEN
Asian, late 20s–early 30s

JENNIFER CHEN
Asian, 30s

RUSS THE BUS/REGGIE/CUSTOMS GUY
white, 30s

TZI CHUAN/MELVIN/DAD/GENERAL TSO
Asian, 40s–60s

THERAPIST/MOM/COUSIN CHEN/MATCHMAKER
Asian, 40s–60s

SETTING

Irvine, America.
And also the Shenzen Special Economic Zone, China.

TIME

Now (circa 2016).

NOTE

Cast Asian actors to play Asian characters. The Chen family is Chinese-American, so casting native English-speaking Chinese-American actors would be ideal. But if those actors aren't available, native English-speaking East Asian/API actors are also acceptable. But if those actors aren't available, stop.

No Chinese accents ever. Not ever.

TIGER STYLE!

ACT ONE

Scene 1. A park.

In the darkness we hear the opening to a song like "Wu Tang Clan Ain't Nuthing ta F' Wit." It gets more insistent until lights come up to birds chirping. Albert's at a park bench. In comes Tzi Chuan. Tzi Chuan notices Albert. Albert notices Tzi Chuan. "Oh shit," thinks Albert, but "oh shit" or not, the Inquisition's begun.*

TZI CHUAN. Hey. *Hey.*

ALBERT. *(Takes out his phone.)* Phone. I'm on…phone call.

TZI CHUAN. You Chinese?

ALBERT. *(To God.)* No. Please? Please no…

TZI CHUAN. *(A challenge.)* No? *Not* Chinese?

ALBERT. Yes, but that doesn't mean we're like *bonded*. I don't wanna do the *thing* where you…

TZI CHUAN. Ahhhh. I'm Chinese too! Tzi Chuan is my name.

ALBERT. I will definitely remember that.

TZI CHUAN. Where are your parents from?

ALBERT. What? From Irvine. My parents were born here in Irvine and my grandparents were born in China okay?

TZI CHUAN. Ah. You were born here.

ALBERT. Yeah I'm third generation. Or whatever.

TZI CHUAN. What do you do?

---

* See Special Note on Songs/Recordings at the back of this volume.

ALBERT. Listen: I was raised to respect my elders so I hope you won't think me a bad Chinese? But I also don't think our shared heritage obligates me to endure a series of penetrating questions from you. Is that *unreasonable*, or...?

TZI CHUAN. Ah?

ALBERT. *(Mimicking.)* Ah.

TZI CHUAN. Ah?

ALBERT. Ah.

TZI CHUAN. Ah?

ALBERT. Don't "ah-ah" me, you know what I'm saying.

TZI CHUAN. *(As though he understands.)* Ah ah ah! *(As before.)* What do you do?

ALBERT. Right, who cares what *I* want... I work for MedCo Medical Software.

TZI CHUAN. *Medical*, ahhh. You're a *doctor*!

> *Albert swallows.*

ALBERT. *No*, I'm a software programmer. Like computers?

TZI CHUAN. Oh, computers! Very good money.

ALBERT. S'not bad.

TZI CHUAN. How much money?

ALBERT. Dude, seriously? *Seventy-five thousand.*

TZI CHUAN. You have siblings, yes?

ALBERT. Yes I live with my older sister Jenny, who is a doctor. Yes, Jenny's a doctor and I'm just a software programmer, *(Affectless.)* ha ha ha ha.
So to reiterate: one older sister—overachieving doctor. One younger brother—smart but lazy software engineer who pulls in a respectable seventy thou. What else you want pal? My social security number? My blood type?

TZI CHUAN. You speak Chinese?

ALBERT. No.

TZI CHUAN. *Chay.* How come you're Chinese you don't...

ALBERT. ...speak Chinese. I know! *But it happened.*

TZI CHUAN. You ever go back to China?

ALBERT. No.

TZI CHUAN. But you *want* to go back.

ALBERT. Not really.

TZI CHUAN. *Chay.* Why don't you want to go back?

ALBERT. Look pal. I don't know who in ancient China came up with this arduous ritual but you need to quit. I'm on my lunch break, okay?!

TZI CHUAN. Ahhhh. Okay sorry, so sorry. Didn't mean to *bother you*, sorry...

    He exits.

ALBERT. I'm not trying to be a jerk, I'm just trying to respect your cultural expectations without letting it bury my personhood. So... thanks for recognizing my personhood, creepy park-walker guy. Oh and my name's *Albert* by the way. Albert? Not that you guys ever ask.

    Russ the Bus enters.

RUSS THE BUS. Ask what Albro?

ALBERT. *(Quick mutter.)* Don't call me Albro.

RUSS THE BUS. Albro what's UP?

ALBERT. What's up with you, Russ the Bus?

RUSS THE BUS. Sweet NOTHIN' man. Russ the Bus is living the DREAM. Yo, who ya talkin' to?

ALBERT. This weird old man, who was racial profiling me, which I hate.

RUSS THE BUS. Not familiar, but I feel you. Hey, quick question—

ALBERT. It's like: Just because you know my race doesn't mean you know *me*. It doesn't mean you get to project your racial assumptions on me as though...

RUSS THE BUS. Hold that rant. I actually *don't* know your race. What are you, Albro?

ALBERT. Still not "Albro."

RUSS THE BUS. Wait, lemme *guess*.

ALBERT. No, my ethnicity's not a party game.

RUSS THE BUS. I got it. Korean? No, Japanese!

ALBERT. No. Please? Please no…

RUSS THE BUS. It's hard cuz your skin tone *says* Filipino but your bone structure *screams* Malaysian. *Wait.* Are you Indonesian? No, no, no. *Peloponnesian?*

ALBERT. You're asking am I from the Greek peninsula of Peloponnesus.

RUSS THE BUS. I got it: You're ethnically Hmong but geographically from the Laotian–Cambodian border.

ALBERT. Russ the Bus: stop.

RUSS THE BUS. Nah-nah, I'll get it. You're Uyghur from Kyrgyzstan.

ALBERT. Russ.

RUSS THE BUS. You're Tibetan raised by Nepalese monks.

ALBERT. Russ.

RUSS THE BUS. You're Vietnamese raised by wolves.

ALBERT. *Russell.*

RUSS THE BUS. And don't say biracial. Do not say biracial, that's cheating.

ALBERT. I'm Chinese okay? Chinese-American.

RUSS THE BUS. Oh. Well that's boring.

ALBERT. Yes it IS boring. So we good here, or…?

RUSS THE BUS. Actually bro-han I got a work question for ya. By any chance have you cracked the UI on the patient data compiler?

ALBERT. "Cracked" it? *Yes* I've "cracked it." I've been slaving over that project all week.

RUSS THE BUS. I know, I was gonna get on that, but it's Friday, you know? Can't do SHIT on a Friday.

ALBERT. My output's pretty consistent regardless of day of the week.

RUSS THE BUS. Man that's because you're a robot. "I am Albro. I am a robot. My output is unaffected regardless of day of the week."

ALBERT. Russ the Bus, you always do this! You seriously haven't been coding? Our team's due for a status report by end of day. Plus it's our annual reviews today!

RUSS THE BUS. Dude, on a *Friday*?

ALBERT. This isn't the *weekend*! If a Friday were part of the weekend they would've called it a Saturday.

RUSS THE BUS. Wait, but if Friday is Saturday, what's Saturday?

ALBERT. Saturday would be…Sunday.

RUSS THE BUS. Then what's—

ALBERT. Sunday would be Sunday Part Two! It doesn't matter because Friday IS Friday so you should've been coding as I have.

RUSS THE BUS. "Coding as I have. I am a Robot."

ALBERT. This time you're really gonna get us in trouble with Melvin.

RUSS THE BUS. Naaaaaah Melvin *loves* Russ the Bus.

ALBERT. Melvin loves diligence. You're jeopardizing our team status report.

RUSS THE BUS. So help out yer boy, nam*sayin*'? Yeahhhh, you know whamsayin'.

ALBERT. Okay, you know something? I was raised to believe in sacrificing my individual needs for the sake of the group. So *fine*. I will give you my code. *Again.*

RUSS THE BUS. That's frickin AWESOME. I'm gonna go take a nap.

ALBERT. I'm not doing this so you can nap!

RUSS THE BUS. *(Singing, like "O Sole Mio.")* "Al-bro-a-mio." Lil buddy: Can Russ the Bus kiss you on the mouth? YOU? Are a lifesaver. Catch ya later Albro!

    He kisses Albert and exits.

ALBERT. My *NAME*. Is Albert!

    Tzi Chuan enters.

TZI CHUAN. Albert. What's your blood type?

Scene 2. Jennifer and Albert's place.

Jennifer kind of invades the scene and all of a sudden we're in her house.

JENNIFER. This isn't happening, Reggie. Three *years*! How can you throw away three years of our lives? We have a good thing going here!

REGGIE. No, Jenny, we *had* a good thing. Until you had to start pressuring me.

JENNIFER. I take it back then. I take back my ultimatum. It was more like an ultimaybe, okay? Like maaaybe we should maybe get married.

REGGIE. I'm not ready to go down that road.

JENNIFER. Is it because of my biological clock? I can change that. I don't need to have babies immediately. Soon though.

REGGIE. I can't *do this*, okay? I can't keep living with you and your brother.

JENNIFER. Is this about Albert? I'll kill him!

REGGIE. I can't keep hiding from your parents.

JENNIFER. You want me to tell them we're dating? Because you know how they feel about that.

REGGIE. I can't have a *baby*.

JENNIFER. You can with my help.

REGGIE. *Yeah*, except I don't *want to*.

JENNIFER. So that's it then. You're dumping me?

REGGIE. Pretty much.

JENNIFER. But… But you can't dump me! I'm a doctor.

REGGIE. See *this* is your whole fuckin' attitude. You're not better than me just because you're a doctor.

JENNIFER. Yes I am.

REGGIE. *Okay.*

JENNIFER. Reggie, you install car radios.

REGGIE. Sound systems.

JENNIFER. Whatever.

REGGIE. No it's not whatever. The sound-systems lifestyle is part of my core values. See: You don't get me. You don't recognize the uniquely compelling individual that I am as a person and that's why I'm not happy.

JENNIFER. Happy? What's happy? Reggie, I was raised to believe that life is about delayed gratification until you've achieved the objectives you've hoped to achieve.

REGGIE. Well I can't live by your irrationally high expectations.

JENNIFER. Even if I have high expectations, I only place them on me. All you have to do is hang on for the ride and not fall off of my back.

REGGIE. That's not true, I feel super pressured by you.

JENNIFER. But you live in my house rent-free.

REGGIE. So? My apartment had black mold.

JENNIFER. I put you on my insurance.

REGGIE. I was fine rolling the dice.

JENNIFER. I even offered to pay for your post-bac!

REGGIE. I don't have time for a post-bac, not with my band!

JENNIFER. I just… Reggie I'm trying to be less demanding here, but it feels like there's literally nothing less to demand.

REGGIE. Stop trying to FIX ME, okay? I got plans for my life.

JENNIFER. *(Derisive.) Plans.* What plans?

REGGIE. Fuckin', like, *plans*. Like going to Bonnaroo.

JENNIFER. But you can't leave me after I sunk so much time into you. I'm on a highly detailed timetable for how I want to live out my life and I have no time for personal hiccups.

REGGIE. Don't call me a hiccup. I am a man!

JENNIFER. I can't believe I'm not the one leaving you! I mean you with your aimlessness and your boxes and boxes of stereo components.

REGGIE. I'll clear out my equipment tomorrow, just rent me the U-Haul.

JENNIFER. No, fuck the equipment…

REGGIE. Whoa whoa whoa, "fuck the equipment"? I'm not leaving without my equipment!

JENNIFER. I have to know why you're leaving *at all.*

REGGIE. Dude, I dunno, I just don't find this relationship fun.

JENNIFER. This relationship isn't *what*? Isn't *fun*? What's *fun*? I haven't had fun my whole life. I graduated Harvard in *three years.* I was the first M.D./Ph.D. ever to sell out a concert at Carnegie Hall. When I started pulling eighteen-hour shifts at the hospital my first thought was *finally some down time*! What do you bring to the picture, ya lazyass? Cuz I'm a clinical oncologist with a perfect survival rate and perfect dentistry. I'm patently awesome!

REGGIE. Yeah on paper maybe. In life you're kind of exhausting.

JENNIFER. Why? Because all you wanna do is have *fun*? *(Mocking.)* Hey everybody, this guy wants to have *fun*. Let's go to the circus! Let's go fly a kite! *(Insta-sad.)* Let's go…let's go throw away the best years of our lives with each other.

REGGIE. Jenny.

> *She sobs.*

Jenny stop. I wasn't even a very good boyfriend!

JENNIFER. I know!

REGGIE. Then WHY do you want me in some kept-man situation?

JENNIFER. I don't know! I thought it was time for a serious committed relationship so I got on OKCupid and we were a ninety-six percent match. Ninety-six percent is an A!

REGGIE. That's…really no basis for a relationship.

JENNIFER. Well what about you, huh? Why'd you get together with me?

REGGIE. I dunno Jenny… It's like, when we first started dating you seemed so *exotic.* But lately you've been totally harshing on me and that sucks. Like I thought you'd be more submissive. And yet also exotically sexy? Like I thought you'd be more domineering in bed yet more submissive around the house.

JENNIFER. …*WHAT*?! How can I be submissive *and* domineering?

REGGIE. I don't know! *Yeah*, it sounds like nonsensical nonsense, *but fuckit*! That's what I think I deserve.

JENNIFER. Well can I work on it? I guess I could be more…submissively domineering for you?

REGGIE. Sorry babe, you had your chance. I'm my own animal now.

    He exits.

JENNIFER. Uh uh uh… Okay, Reggie, well have a *fun life*. Have *fun* while I'm at the hospital every day SAVING LIVES. And for the record? You're a man-child with a cinderblock for a brain and a coal for a heart, your hair's thin, your dick's thin, and as a former concert pianist with absolute pitch let me just say? Your car stereos have flimsy electrical cords and they overemphasize subwoofer capacity at the expense of acoustical balance SO THERE.

Scene 3. Albert's office.

    The scene shifts to Albert's office, with Albert sliding in on a rolly chair.

MELVIN. You ready Albert?

ALBERT. Oh hey Melvin, sure.

MELVIN. Albert this annual review will be brief. You're doing okay, your output's okay, and I really don't have any feedback one way or the other. However I do want to inform you that MedCo will be modifying the reporting tree.

ALBERT. Got it.

MELVIN. A little less lateral and a little more hierarchical.

ALBERT. Got it, so does this mean I'm getting a raise?!

MELVIN. What?

ALBERT. Oh shit. Does this mean I'm fired?

MELVIN. Albert hold on.

ALBERT. Omigod does this mean…omigod what does this MEAN?

MELVIN. This means very little in terms of your daily workflow. I'm just promoting some of our team members to mid-level leadership status.

13

ALBERT. So this means…

MELVIN. You'll now be reporting to Russell.

ALBERT. *Russ the Bus?* You're giving a promotion to Russ the Bus?

MELVIN. Correct.

ALBERT. *Ummmm.* Could I offer some constructive three-sixty-degree feedback?

MELVIN. *(Weary.)* What's that Albert?

ALBERT. I'm not so sure you should promote Russ the Bus. *(Confidential.)* Russ the Bus is kind of an idiot.

MELVIN. Albert, there's no grounds for name-calling.

ALBERT. Oh no, oh no, that's not name-calling, that's an objective assessment. I'm only thinking of what's best for MedCo.

MELVIN. What'd be best for MedCo is if we adopt the reporting tree and get back to work.

ALBERT. *Yeahhh*, it's just… I've been here twice as long as Russ the Bus.

MELVIN. I'm aware of that Albert.

ALBERT. I went to Harvard. Russ the Bus went to the University of Phoenix online.

MELVIN. I'm sorry, but there's nothing I can do.

ALBERT. What? No, you're the one doing this. You're the one giving him the promotion.

MELVIN. *Okay? (I.e. "Meaning what?")*

ALBERT. Here's a thing you can do: Promote me instead.

MELVIN. No, see, when I said there's nothing I can do what I meant is I can't do that.

ALBERT. Okay okay but can you—not in any way to malign your judgment here—but can you maybe just give me some insights into your reasoning so I can bear it in mind for the future?

MELVIN. Yeah sure, I just think Russell's a really good guy. I find him very relatable.

ALBERT. *Relatable.* But but but I'm the only one who does any *work.* You do know that all of our output comes from my code?

MELVIN. There's nothing from your project reports to suggest that.

ALBERT. That's because we're a team. I never talk about myself on reports because we're supposed to work as a team.

MELVIN. Yes, Albert, you're a very good worker. But I'm just not sure you're a leader.

ALBERT. That's because I'm a reluctant leader! I'm like the world-weary hero who only leads when he's called on. Like Achilles in the *Iliad*. Or Eminem in *Eight Mile*.

MELVIN. I just haven't seen it.

ALBERT. That's because you're supposed to coax it out of me, Melvin. In fact maybe the fact that you didn't coax out my leadership skills illustrates your failure in leadership.

MELVIN. Albert this whole conversation demonstrates you have no communication skills.

> *Melvin starts to exit.*

ALBERT. Actions speak louder than words. You know Chinese people don't brag.

MELVIN. What does being Chinese have to do with this?

ALBERT. Because! Like… Come on man. You're Asian.

MELVIN. What does THAT have to do with anything?

ALBERT. It means we're s'posed to look out for each other.

MELVIN. No. I don't do that.

ALBERT. Come on, don't be a self-hating Asian, be a nepotistic Asian. How you gonna call Russ the Bus more relatable when you 'n' me are same-same? We gotta look out for each other my brothaaaaa.

MELVIN. Albert stop. Stop using race as a crutch.

ALBERT. It isn't a crutch! A crutch would help me to *get* somewhere.

MELVIN. This is pure meritocracy here.

ALBERT. *Meritocracy?* He goes by RUSS THE BUS.

> *Albert swallows, then coughs. And coughs. He coughs into a napkin. It's a little bit weird.*

MELVIN. Albert go home. You need a day off to calm down.

ALBERT. Oh I'm super-calm. I'm Zen as fuck.

MELVIN. Can you at least take a break? You're bugging me out.

ALBERT. I can't do that sir. We have a team status report due end of day. Now if you'll excuse me.

Russ the Bus bursts in.

RUSS THE BUS. Wooooo! Albro did you hear the good news? I'm gonna be your boss! Fetch me a coffee motherfucka! How many sugars? One hump or two?

He starts humping Albert.

Yeah Yeah Yeah Yeah!

Pause, looks around.

Is this a bad time?

Scene 4. Albert and Jennifer's place.

Scene-shift around Albert. Jennifer is lying in fetal position. She emits a low guttural moan.

ALBERT. Are we gonna talk about this?

JENNIFER. What's there to talk about? I'm a failure, you're a failure, let's all get fetal about it.

ALBERT. It's during tough times like these I hear Mom and Dad's comforting words. What were they? That's right: "Suck it up."

JENNIFER. You suck it up.

ALBERT. Reggie was objectively *TURRIBLE*.

JENNIFER. Don't you think I know that? He goes, "Hey I wanna be a complete useless bum," and I go, "That's cool, I'll just store up that small modicum of affection you once showed for me and use it like nuclear fuel to power this relationship 'til the day that I die." Don't you think I hate myself for that?

ALBERT. Good. Then we've learned something.

JENNIFER. No, because I miss him like crazy! I want him so bad my heart's gonna explode. If he came back now covered in dogshit with two child brides, I'd still be like, "Fuckit, I'll take it." But that's normal, right? Tell me what I'm feeling is normal.

ALBERT. It's abnormal.

JENNIFER. Oh, you're the worst…

ALBERT. You were a hundred times better than Reggie. You paired with Reggie was a *stark* example of market inefficiencies, and that bugs me from an arbitrage standpoint.

JENNIFER. Albert, you're a robot! You're an emotionless robot! Try some sympathy maybe!

ALBERT. No, you grow a backbone. You're a highly put-together professional woman. Why would you settle for dirt?

JENNIFER. Because I'm a very busy physician. Because Mom and Dad forbid us from dating 'til we got out of school, which means I had no idea what a healthy relationship looks like. Because Mom always said that a daughter shouldn't make waves, so I felt like I had to make do with the man that I had.

ALBERT. You sound like Amy Tan.

JENNIFER. Fuck off! Like *you've* got it all figured out. You who's never had a relationship.

ALBERT. I have the internet.

JENNIFER. You who's never had a promotion.

ALBERT. Me and Melvin are working it out.

JENNIFER. You wanna talk about arbitrage? Well let me arbitrage you.

ALBERT. You're not using that word right.

JENNIFER. Instead of being all humble pie Asian, why didn't you confront Melvin with all your achievements?

ALBERT. *Because.* My efforts should speak for themselves. That's what Dad taught us. Dad always said that the cream will rise to the top.

JENNIFER. So then why haven't *you* creamed up?

ALBERT. Ew.

JENNIFER. Ew, sorry, I hear it now. Anyway your professional life is in shambles and if you had any self-respect you'd be angry.

ALBERT. Oh I don't have to be angry. I don't act like a sad sack like you, barfing out my emotions. Instead I practice the Eastern values of stoicism, equanimity.

JENNIFER. Practice them *how*?!

ALBERT. It's a Zen thing. Whenever I feel myself getting angry I just swallow.

JENNIFER. That doesn't sound like a Zen thing. That sounds like a stupid thing you made up.

ALBERT. It's just how I deal with things. See?

> *He swallows, he exhales, he coughs blood.*

JENNIFER. Oh my God is that blood? You have an ULCER you stupid shit. You have an ulcer from holding things in!

ALBERT. You don't know. What are you, a doctor? Fine, you're a doctor, but not a good one.

JENNIFER. Look at this!

> *She pokes his stomach.*

ALBERT. Owwwww.

> *Pause.*

Whatever, this is fine. I'll just get the ulcer to hold in its anger from being an ulcer, and then the ulcer will form a mini-ulcer, and the mini-ulcer will hold that in, and so on and so on until there's no blood.

JENNIFER. You're an idiot.

ALBERT. *(An outburst.)* Russ the Bus is an idiot! Russ the Bus is a mouth-breathing idiot!

> *Pause.*

You know maybe I am angry. I don't know what to do with all these preconceptions people hold about us as Asians!

JENNIFER. I thought we were talking about personal problems.

ALBERT. Um. My boss says I'm not *relatable*. Your boyfriend called you exotic. These are racialized code words.

JENNIFER. I could be exotic?

ALBERT. Right, the Chinese-American Ivy Leaguer who went into medicine? You're the fuckin' *vanilla ice cream* of Asians… Look, it's not like I *want* to view everything through the context of race, but this is the context that's shoved upon us before we even get to decide. *And Yet* when people talk about *race* in this country they only mean black and white issues, so where does that leave room for us? It's no wonder my body's eating me up inside.

JENNIFER. Jeez Mom and Dad always said if we worked hard and didn't make waves, race wouldn't be an issue.

ALBERT. Of course they'd say that. I told Mom I wanted to take an Asian-American studies class? She said, "If you want to study Asians you can look in a mirror for free."

JENNIFER. "Hi I'm Dad. Merry Christmas Jenny. Have a savings bond! You'll thank me in twenty years."

ALBERT. "Uh son? You need MORE rosin for your cello? Why don't you buy some using your nonexistent allowance. *Responsibility!* Fuh fuh fuh."

JENNIFER. "Don't talk to boys Jenny, don't talk to boys. Hey what's the holdup on grandkids?"

ALBERT. You know something Jenny? This is all Mom and Dad's fault! Their whole life philosophy's cocked. All that college prep. All that SAT prep. Mom and Dad were tiger-parenting tyrants!

JENNIFER. Wait, no, I wouldn't go that far. Mom and Dad were more like benevolent dictators, harnessing our youthful potential. Because of them I was top of my class from grade school through med school.

ALBERT. Me too. Minus the med school.

JENNIFER. Plus all that concert piano.

ALBERT. Concert cello.

JENNIFER. We sold out a concert at Carnegie Hall! That's gotta mean something.

ALBERT. I haven't touched a cello in years. It's not like those *thousands* of hours of practice have any practical value. Like, "Omigod this man's choking." Good thing I'm a cellist! "Omigod there's a gun to my head." Good thing I'm a cellist! "Omigod there's nobody flying the plane!"

JENNIFER. Albert: If you haven't capitalized on your talents that's not Mom and Dad's fault.

ALBERT. Yes it is, because they should've taught you some self-respect. Now you're just one of those low-self-esteem Asians who substitutes professional growth for personal growth.

JENNIFER. Don't call me a low-self-esteem Asian! I'm a *doctor*! *(Realizes.)* Ohhhh I get it. *(Recovers.)* Fine well *you—you're* just one of those pushover Asians who can't stand up for yourself at work so you go home and yell at your family.

ALBERT. Fuck you Jenny I hate you!! *(Realizes.)* Ohhh I get it too… There, you see? Mom and Dad gave us NO LIFE SKILLS. That's the real reason you got dumped.

JENNIFER. Yeah? So it wasn't my judgmental rigidity?

ALBERT. Who else do we know who's judgmental and rigid?

JENNIFER. Oh my god, Albert, you're right!

ALBERT. Damn right I'm right. So I say we drive out to San Marino, tell Mom and Dad what we really think of their parenting, and demand an apology.

JENNIFER. I'm not going to stuffy-ass *Chan* Marino. That's like a two-hour drive off the 5 to the 605.

ALBERT. We have to. Yelling at our parents is the only way we can shed our old hangups and move on to be full-grown adults. This is what everyone else does!

JENNIFER. Yeah, but *we* don't do that. We're supposed to respect our elders. Plus I can't bloody well blame Mom and Dad for the live-in boyfriend that they've never met.

ALBERT. Oh but you will. *Secrets will be revealed that threaten to tear the family apart.*

JENNIFER. Wait why are you saying that like that? Where have I heard that?

ALBERT. Oh every year we get a brochure from that theater and that's what all their shows are about. Uhhhh—

> *Albert fishes through mail.*

—see?

JENNIFER. Oh yeah… Coming in December: The Van Fussburgs reunite at their cabin in coastal Maine, until an old stranger drops by. *Secrets will be revealed that threaten to tear the family apart.* Coming in January: The McMillicents are having a dinner party in their Tribeca loft, but not all is as it seems. *Secrets will be revealed that threaten to tear the family apart.* Coming in February: *Fences* by August Wilson. Coming in March…

ALBERT. So will you do it? The Chen family reunites in stuffy-ass San Marino but Jennifer's gotta come clean. Secrets will…

JENNIFER. Secrets will be revealed that threaten to—got it. I'll only do this if you do it too.

ALBERT. Oh you better believe I'll do it. I'm gonna yell at my mom like a white girl.

JENNIFER. This could be downright therapeutic. Instigating a fight with our family sounds like a full and satisfying evening of entertainment.

ALBERT. Way ahead of you, calling them now.

   He gets on the phone.

Hello Mom? We wanted to stop by for dinner tonight, is that cool? Yeah, both of us, yeah! Do you think you could make us some mapo doufu? Yeah maybe some mapo doufu and some bok choy and also a side of *secrets will be / revealed that threaten to tear the family apart!*

JENNIFER. *Secrets will be revealed that threaten to tear the family apart!*

Scene 5. Mom and Dad's house.

A very patrician house with wine-swilling, well-to-do parents.

MOM. It's such a pleasant surprise you stopped by!

JENNIFER. It's a—it WILL be a surprise.

DAD. *(Chipper.)* Well okay!

MOM. You know I had a faculty meeting at UCLA but I thought—heck, I can postpone that. Family's much more important.

DAD. Hey what do you think of a Bordeaux? Will that go with black bean sauce?

MOM. Ask Albert what he thinks.

DAD. Pairing wine with Chinese food is such an impossible task, but I try.

MOM. Speaking of Albert, where did he go?

> *WHAM! Albert comes in with a moving box filled to the brim.*

Honey what's this?

ALBERT. Oh that? That's every last award-winning science fair project and spelling bee certificate and academic decathlon trophy, every last scrap of my academic achievement because it means NOTHING now. NOTHING.

DAD. Oh so you finally cleaned out your room? Terrific.

ALBERT. Dad. Big revelation headed right at ya: I didn't get a promotion. At work.

DAD. Okay…

ALBERT. I failed Dad. I got passed up by a fuckwit.

DAD. Well that stinks.

ALBERT. Yeah it does stink. So whaddya think about it, huh? I didn't live up to your high expectations. Aren't you going to yell at me for it?

DAD. Well it sounds like you didn't live up to your own expectations. So why would I yell.

ALBERT. Okay okay fine. So you're cool with it huh? Everyone's cool? You want secrets? Well Jen's got the bomb secret. Jen, drop the bomb.

JENNIFER. Mom. Dad. I had a secret live-in boyfriend for three years and we didn't tell you. And then he dumped me. And. And! It's all *your fault.*

ALBERT. BOOM SUCKA. Secrets will be revealed.

JENNIFER. So what do you think Ma?

MOM. That's a pretty dumb secret. Why would you go to such pains to hide your boyfriend?

JENNIFER. What does it matter? You wouldn't have liked him anyway because he wasn't Chinese.

MOM. What am I, a bigot?

JENNIFER. Yeah probably.

MOM. Honey, I'm not. I don't care about the color of somebody's skin.

DAD. That's right, honey, we don't.

MOM. I do care what *job* he has.

JENNIFER. Car radio fixer.

MOM. You got together with a *car radio fixer*?! Are you outta your mind? You're a doctor.

JENNIFER. There, you see? This is exactly what I knew you would do! I knew you'd judge him so that's why I judged him too, and that's precisely what pushed him away.

ALBERT. Ipso facto, he dumped her ass.

JENNIFER. Which is your fault.

ALBERT. But also kind of okay cuz the dude was straight-up terrible.

JENNIFER. So. Are you mad?

DAD. We're not *mad*, we're just disappointed.

MOM. And hurt! We really don't like it when you keep things from us.

ALBERT. That's because you're Gestapo. You always want every detail of our lives.

JENNIFER. So you can judge all our choices.

ALBERT. You used to say shit like, "Albert, we have a lot of friends in the community, so I'd better hear it from you before I hear it from them." That's a Gestapo tactic!

MOM. We just want to be included and for that we're *Gestapo*?

DAD. We like knowing what's going on with you because we're very tight-knit.

JENNIFER. No we're not! I hid this guy for three years!

MOM. Well it sounds like you hid him because you were ashamed of him. So maybe it's good that he dumped you.

JENNIFER. But!

DAD. And how can you say we're not tight-knit? You're over for dinner.

JENNIFER. But for a reckoning.

DAD. You also live with your brother.

ALBERT. That's for tax purposes!

MOM. I see. So we are to blame for a guy that we've never met.

JENNIFER. Because high expectations! And always having us working.

ALBERT. See no time for social skills. Look how awkward she is.

JENNIFER. Not helpful!

DAD. And we're to blame for your lack of promotion as well.

ALBERT. Hell yeah because you raised us both to be DICKLESS.

MOM. *Albert!*

ALBERT. We're all of us dickless Asians!

JENNIFER. I'm actually okay being dickless…

ALBERT. No, but why did you train us to be so deferential if it means that Jennifer let her dumb boyfriend treat her like a doormat? And why do I let people treat me like a doormat? Plus I'm yelling right now! I'm yelling! Why are you letting us treat you like doormats?!

DAD. So stop yelling already!

ALBERT. We're fuckups! Yell at us for it! This was supposed to be a reckoning! A night where secrets get…something something. Ahhhhh!

    Cough cough cough.

MOM. Is that blood? Jennifer why aren't you taking care of your brother?

JENNIFER. Me take care of him? I can't even take care of myself!

ALBERT. You didn't give us the preparation we needed to face the world! Don't you think you owe us an apology?

JENNIFER. Yeah!

DAD. I beg your pardon.

ALBERT. You really put the screws to us. We basically had no childhood.

MOM. Of course you had a childhood!

ALBERT. A childhood of flashcards and workbooks and extra

summer school and for WHAT? They started cheating off my tests in middle school and it pretty much hasn't stopped since.

JENNIFER. Yeah, you made it seem like everything would blossom from hard work and education. That people would respect me for my career. So how come no one respects us?

ALBERT. Why'd we waste so much time in an academia arms race if the world runs on buddy-buddy networks you never acknowledged exist?

JENNIFER. You had us practicing our stupid music all day like it meant something. We had the metronome running *for hours* and-now-I-have-be-come-one. What for?

ALBERT. Well? Well? Can't you see that it's all your fault?

DAD. I'm sorry, but all of this? Sounds like a whole lotta *your fault*.

MOM. Damn right.

DAD. You want an apology? Try prying one out of my cold dead throat.

MOM. This is *our house*. Take your shoes off outside and leave your attitude out there as well.

DAD. You want to know why we insisted on your education?

MOM. We gave you the best education we could, so that you'd never be poor like we were.

JENNIFER. That's *it*?

DAD. Whaddya mean "that's it"? I grew up in the ghetto.

ALBERT. We worked ourselves to the bone to get here. We didn't do it just to avoid poverty, we should be kicking some serious ass.

DAD. What does kicking ass mean to you? You have a job, you own property. You have your family, your health…

ALBERT. Nah-nah-nah, don't feed me that American Dream crap. After three generations in this country I don't want the American Dream. I wanna be an American *Idiot* with all the irrational self-confidence and sense of entitlement such a position of privilege entails.

JENNIFER. Yeah and I want the American rom-com where I can have it all, cuz by now I think that I've earned it.

DAD. Okay, well Albert. If you want to win you'll have to work twice as hard, like we did.

ALBERT. But why not *as hard*.

MOM. And Jennifer: If you wanna not fall into terrible relationships, *don't*. It's as simple as that.

JENNIFER. But—but what about all these conflicting emotions that go into *why* I would do that?

MOM. I dunno. Fix it. Who has time for all of this weepy-weepy? They don't give you enough to do at that oncology department if you're asking me.

JENNIFER. But aren't you going to tell us what to do?

DAD. No. We can't live your lives for you.

JENNIFER. But that's exactly what you used to do!

MOM. Yes but all of that browbeating stops when you get out of school.

JENNIFER. Why? That's so arbitrary.

MOM. Honey, Chinese families are tight, tight enough to be separated by continents and not lose sight of our love. But our love is a tough love because when you're separated by continents you can't molly-coddle your babies. You have to give your children the training they need to figure things out on their own.

JENNIFER. But we haven't figured out shit!

ALBERT. Plus, like, we're on the same continent *now*, what the fuck?

DAD. So our old-world values have failed you. So sue us.

MOM. You think I *wanted* to proof all your papers? Drive you to all those recitals and science competitions? You think it was fun for me drilling multiplication tables with you? I know damn well how to multiply. It's parents who *don't care* about their kids who would choose not to bother with that.

JENNIFER. Look your methods obviously worked, to a point. We're not renouncing the tools you gave us. We just need more tools.

DAD. Jenny do me a favor. Take down that photo of my parents.

JENNIFER. What, this?

She takes a photo down from the wall.

26

DAD. Yeah. That. That's a photo of my parents on Angel Island. Your grandfather came here in 1936 under a fake name. He was a paper son—he used all his money to buy some fake papers and used a fake name to enter the U.S. and make a better life for his family. He left your grandma in China with their oldest daughter—my sister, you've never even met her, she died over there. You want to talk about unfair? There was a *quota* on the number of Chinese who could immigrate to the States, so your grandma was stranded in China even though any old European fella could get naturalized with his wife, his three kids, and seventeen cousins. But your grandfather was college-educated. His future was bright. So he applied to the best job he could get: as a dishwasher. Oh, that's right. You wanna talk about *unfair*. In those days the Chinese were systematically passed over for white-collar jobs. So he kept washing dishes and sending money back to China until his *big break* came: working at a fucking laundry. And by the time your grandparents were reunited fifteen years later he owned that laundry. Your grandparents became small-business owners and they had nothing to start from—not even their real name. I'm an engineer now but I come from laundry people. Your mom is a chemist by way of some cabbage farmers.

MOM. I had to work two waitressing jobs to put myself through UCLA. But hey. I'm sure if my mother wasn't so busy with *grueling farm labor* she'd have given me an *apology*.

DAD. Kids, I hate to break it to you but we've done our job. You two have every advantage we could provide. We didn't ask our parents for additional tools and neither will you.

JENNIFER. Can I keep this?

DAD. What, the photo of my parents? Hell no, that's my photo.

JENNIFER. Dad, I just…it's so hard navigating this life and I…couldn't just a *little* emotional support and understanding be warranted here instead of continued hard-assery?

MOM. Nope, suck it up.

ALBERT. Right, "suck it up." Let's all keep overcompensating for a flawed, biased system rather than confronting the system itself.

MOM. Albert. As parents? We can't control the system. We can't change the *world*. All we can change is you.

JENNIFER. This is the worst apology ever!

ALBERT. Hold on Jenny I got this.

JENNIFER. Got what?

ALBERT. Okay, so here's where I'm at. I'm thinking maybe Mom and Dad raised us in old-world America but this is new-world America and maybe if we speak up for ourselves we won't get deported anymore so maybe we shouldn't be doormats.

JENNIFER. Dude what are you saying?

ALBERT. I'm saying I've been to the nerd mountaintop and that mountain is empty!

JENNIFER. Dude I still don't know what you're saying.

ALBERT. I'm saying that I have a dream. A dream not to change the world because Mom says we can't so let's not even try. I have a dream of changing ourselves! To not be such dickless Asians! I'm saying let's go on an Asian Freedom Tour! Who's with me?

DAD. Nobody is with you! What are you talking about?

Albert gets on the table à la Raisin in the Sun.

ALBERT. I'm talkin' 'bout LIFE. From now on we will no longer be torn between two conflicting traditions. From now on we cut out the meek mild Eastern and go *Full Western*. That is our *right* because this is where we were born.

JENNIFER. Yeah!

DAD. Get down from there, this is rare forest hardwood.

ALBERT. You can't stuff me in a tidy lacquer box of Eastern passivity.

JENNIFER. No, no, ladies.

ALBERT. I'm gonna *get mine. Amurca!*

JENNIFER. *Amurca!* Get Some! I'm a cowboy! Pew pew! Pew pew!

ALBERT. *(Hops down.)* Jen from now on we are gonna be like Bonnie and Clyde!

JENNIFER. Yeah, really?

ALBERT. Fuck ya really. Like I'm gonna march into MedCo and demand the promotion I've earned. Like *demand* it!

JENNIFER. Okay, okay, so if we're going Full Western what do I do?

ALBERT. I dunno, fuck some shit up.

JENNIFER. What if I update my online dating profile?

ALBERT. Go *bigger*.

JENNIFER. Okay okay what if I go see a therapist? *Scary!*

MOM. Oh for God's sake.

JENNIFER. Okay okay okay what if I become an undercover agent who enters a beauty pageant to root out criminals?

MOM. That's the plot to *Miss Congeniality*!

JENNIFER. MAYBE!

ALBERT. Okay we're gonna keep working on what going Full Western would look like for you.

JENNIFER. I'm on it!

MOM. *What* are you *on* exactly?

JENNIFER. I don't know. I'm bummed out that you don't have any answers. Plus we carpooled.

ALBERT. Enough of this nonsense. The Asian Freedom Tour begins. To the Kia Sedona!

> *He exits.*

MOM. But what about dinner?! I bought you the tofu.

JENNIFER. This is *America* Ma! Where we're going we don't need any tofu.

> *She exits.*

DAD. We should've adopted from Africa.

Scene 6. Split scene.

RUSS THE BUS. Albro! Buddy I didn't see any updates from you on the patient data compiler.

ALBERT. Ohhh riiiight. I didn't get to that yet.

RUSS THE BUS. Well when're you gonna get to it? It's three o'clock, lil bro. I gotta be out by Nap-Thirty.

ALBERT. Could I get an extension?

RUSS THE BUS. Sure how long you need?

ALBERT. How about you wait until *never*.

RUSS THE BUS. Albro, what the…what's the idea here?

ALBERT. Oh I'm fresh out of ideas. I'm *American*. I don't have to have any ideas, just unbridled confidence. I've been actively lazy allll day because I'm just as Western as you.

RUSS THE BUS. Okay, time for some manager real-talk. Albro, the only reason I took this promotion was because I thought we were cool with you working a great deal and me *shaping that work* for shared credit.

ALBERT. *Yeah.* About that promotion, Russ the Bus.

RUSS THE BUS. Sir Russ the Bus.

ALBERT. What?

RUSS THE BUS. I think you should call me sir.

>   *Albert contains himself.*

ALBERT. No.

RUSS THE BUS. What d'you mean "no"?

ALBERT. Why should I call you "sir" when you call me "Albro"?

RUSS THE BUS. What's wrong with "Albro"?

ALBERT. I NEVER liked Albro!

RUSS THE BUS. Why not? You're my little bro.

ALBERT. I am not your little brother. I'm older than you, I've been here longer than you, and I'm smarter than you.

RUSS THE BUS. But you're so *little*.

ALBERT. God damn it Russ the Bus I may be cute as a button but inside me is a very grizzled very very angry adult.

RUSS THE BUS. Whoa man.

ALBERT. No YOU whoa man. YOU.

RUSS THE BUS. Yo but what am I whoa-ing?

ALBERT. Russ the Bus, I need a raise.

RUSS THE BUS. Yo I don't know.

ALBERT. More to the point, Russ the Bus, I need your job.

RUSS THE BUS. Yo what?

ALBERT. You heard me dum-dum, I need your job. And you're gonna give it to me.

> *Lights shift to Jennifer at a therapist's office.*

THERAPIST. Jennifer?

JENNIFER. Hi. Hi hi hi there. Thanks for seeing me. I'm brand new to therapy.

THERAPIST. Of course. Have a seat.

JENNIFER. Okay so LET'S DO THIS! Full Western! I stayed up all night.

THERAPIST. Why would you have to?

JENNIFER. This is a list of my phobias. And this is a list of my traumas. There's not very many, I had a *very* good childhood, so there's not a whole lot to unearth.

THERAPIST. Jennifer.

JENNIFER. Thiiiis is a list of my shortcomings and a list of my positive attributes. As you can see the shortcomings list is much longer which may point to some self-esteem issues.

THERAPIST. Jennifer if we could just…

JENNIFER. These are my tax returns. Dunno if you need that.

THERAPIST. Jennifer let's step back for a minute.

JENNIFER. Yeah, but we've only got forty-five minutes. We gotta move quick.

THERAPIST. No no, this is just our first session. There's no time pressure here.

JENNIFER. But I'm on a highly detailed timetable for how I want to live out my life.

THERAPIST. And we can talk about that.

JENNIFER. This is the first of how many sessions?

THERAPIST. Oh. Well that's up to you.

JENNIFER. No but you tell me because I like to plan things out. If I know how many sessions in total I can think about what percentage *per session* I'm opening up.

THERAPIST. Hey, here's something. Why don't you go ahead and sit down?

She doesn't.

JENNIFER. Okay, but the lists…

THERAPIST. That's great. So putting aside these lists…

JENNIFER. I need those! *(Re-centers.)* It's fine. I'm fine. I can talk about my feelings and look weak to strangers.

THERAPIST. Let's talk about why you're really here. The problem isn't contained in some homework assignments. It's somewhere in you. Where is it Jen? Point to where it is in the body.

JENNIFER. *(Points to her head.)* Up here?

THERAPIST. No it's lower than that.

JENNIFER. Low—*lower?* *(Points to her crotch.)*

THERAPIST. Jennifer: It's in here. *(Indicates her own heart.)* That's why we don't need the lists.

JENNIFER. But that's how I process. That's the *only* way to process.

THERAPIST. Oh I get it. You're one of *those.*

JENNIFER. One of those what?

THERAPIST. Nothing. Go on.

JENNIFER. I thought my life was on track. But the past few years have been off track. So I need you to get me on track as quickly as possible. My life plan is to find a husband, get a clinical teaching position, save up enough to move out of the share I co-own with my brother, pop out a couple of kids, train them to get in to Harvard, and then retire in Paris after winning the National Medal of Science.

THERAPIST. What about being happy?

JENNIFER. Heh? *(I.e. "Huh?" but "Heh" sounds better.)*

THERAPIST. I noticed you don't mention being happy as part of your life plan.

JENNIFER. So tell me what I should do. Like my mom used to do. Oh hey, I want you to do what my mom did—that's transference right?! I looked up Freud on my phone.

THERAPIST. I'm not a Freudian analyst.

JENNIFER. Okay but given the prep work I've done am I going faster than normal?

THERAPIST. Therapy's not about speed.

JENNIFER. I want to be the BEST at therapy. THE ABSOLUTE BEST.

    Lights shift.

MELVIN. Albert I trust you know why Russell called me here.

RUSS THE BUS. He's freaking me out man! He's having a freak-out.

ALBERT. I'm not having a freak-out.

RUSS THE BUS. Lookit him, Melvin, lookit how freaky-outy he is!

ALBERT. How come when I raise my voice I'm having a freak-out? How come you're allowed to say what you want but I can't?

MELVIN. If Russell says you're having a freak-out, you're having a freak-out.

ALBERT. Why though?

MELVIN. Don't talk to me that way!

ALBERT. What way? What did I say?

MELVIN. Don't raise your voice with me!

ALBERT. What the…? I'm not.

MELVIN. That's it! I'm tired of this. The promotions issue is closed. Everyone get back to work.

    Albert stands tall.

ALBERT. No.

RUSS THE BUS. Uh-oh.

MELVIN. *(Squaring up to Albert.)* Excuse me?

ALBERT. I saaaaaaaid. Nyyyyyoooooooohhhhh.

RUSS THE BUS. Oh my gaaaaawd. It's gonna be like two little Godzillas in here…

    Lights shift.

THERAPIST. Jennifer I can't tell you what to do. But you also can't shortcut your feelings by intellectualizing the problem. You're going through a breakup. You're grieving.

JENNIFER. Yeah but when do I *stop* grieving? Why is this taking so long?

THERAPIST. This breakup happened when?

JENNIFER. Yesterday.

THERAPIST. Jennifer. Being analyzed is not a quick process. It's not some standardized test with standardized answers.

JENNIFER. Yes but I'm a highly analytical person. Which means that I'm A) self-aware and B) highly self-actualized.

THERAPIST. You're neither of those.

JENNIFER. Okay well can you de-program me from my sense of Chinese dutifulness? I feel like my sense of duty to family and culture is smothering the unfettered all-American girl that's inside. So if you could just *conk that out.* Through hypnosis or something!

THERAPIST. Jennifer.

JENNIFER. I just want to be in a rom-com, y'know? I feel like in rom-coms if you're all wound up some guy opens you up to the fact you've had love all along, and then you get to make out with Channing Tatum. When do I get to make out with Channing Tatum? I've been working my ass off!

THERAPIST. I feel that we're getting off track.

JENNIFER. No but help me become the hapless heroine who stumbles backwards into everything that I want. Why can't I be a helpless waify loon? It's because I'm too *competent*, right?

THERAPIST. It's because you're not *in* a rom-com.

JENNIFER. And why's *that*? Is it because I'm *Asian* and there are no Asians in rom-coms?

THERAPIST. Asians in *rom-coms*? WOW Jennifer, your expectations are totally unrealistic.

JENNIFER. Jesus I thought that you'd *get me.* I chose you because I thought you'd be a kindred spirit, right, Doctor? Can I call you Doctor?

THERAPIST. You can't, actually. Well technically you can. I'm a Ph.D. and not an M.D.

JENNIFER. Oh… *Oh.*

THERAPIST. Is that going to be a problem?

JENNIFER. I thought you were a doctor like me.

THERAPIST. It doesn't mean I can't listen, it just means I can't prescribe drugs.

JENNIFER. *I* can prescribe drugs. I'm a doctor. Crap what if I'm *too smart* for therapy.

THERAPIST. Jennifer, no. Smart people are great for analysis. They're really able to get to the truth of…

JENNIFER. Don't use compliments to placate me.

THERAPIST. Jennifer. We have to…

JENNIFER. Stop using my name to establish a bond.

THERAPIST. What would you prefer we do?

JENNIFER. Stop using deflecty questions to put the focus on me. I told you, I'm smart.

THERAPIST. The fallacy here is that you're trying to navigate complex human relationships using solely IQ, whereas EQ is just as important.

JENNIFER. Right IQ is meaningless! I guess I just *wasted* my time becoming an M.D./Ph.D. board-certified double-Harvard-trained doctor.

THERAPIST. Ugh, I can't stand this. You wanna know what you are? You're one of those careerist *dragon ladies* who thinks you're better than me just because you have an M.D. Well if that's your attitude I'm not the one to wake you up to the fact you're completely closed off from what you actually want. Not even Einstein could do that. Who by the way did not have an M.D. either.

    Lights shift.

MELVIN. Look you piece of shit, I'm tired of your attitude.

ALBERT. Too bad, cuz I'm a loose cannon. I'm not your coolie, I'm Cool Hand Luke. And I'm not a team player anymore, I'm playing for ME so you better show me the money, Melvin. Show me the Money!

MELVIN. You know what DJ Yella? No one's buying your cowboy act, okay *Shanghai Noon*? Am I right Russell?

RUSS THE BUS. *(Vastly uncomfortable.)* Yeaaaah…

MELVIN. *Yeah see?* This is America and we don't wanna hear any complaints out of *you*. If you don't like it here you can go back where you came from.

RUSS THE BUS. Woof.

ALBERT. What did you say?

MELVIN. You heard me *Dong Wang*. Go back where you came from!

RUSS THE BUS. K, I'm gonna, I'm just gonna…

He runs away.

ALBERT. Yo. Yoooooo. That's so fucked up. Dude, *you're Asian*. How you gonna say "go back where you came from" to someone else Asian?

MELVIN. You are making us *look bad* in front of Russell. I'm embarrassed to be associated with you.

ALBERT. Well the fact you want to impress *Russ the Bus* makes me embarrassed for ALL OF ASIA.

MELVIN. You know something Albert? People like *you*? Who bring up race as though it's still even an issue? Are fucking it up for the rest of us who just want to live our lives.

ALBERT. I'm not idly bringing up race so much as pointing to vast social inequities and how cultural context creates disparate lenses for valuing people. It's a much subtler inquiry than "bringing up race"—but whatever. Would not bringing up race make you more comfortable, Melvin?

MELVIN. What would make me more comfortable. Is if you go back where you came from.

ALBERT. All right well thanks for your feedback and here is some feedback for you.

He pours a Coke onto his laptop. The laptop sparks and sputters.

MELVIN. What—what are you DOING?

ALBERT. Good luck trying to get Russ the Bus or anyone else on this floor to program the rest of the code for you…*bitch*.

Lights shift.

THERAPIST. Jennifer. If all you want to do is get a rise out of me to prove how smart you are, why are you here?

JENNIFER. Because Albert says we're going Full Western!

THERAPIST. That's barely a sentence. What does that mean?

JENNIFER. I don't frickin know!!

THERAPIST. I think you do know why you're here. You may have some elaborate life plan, but that plan is making you miserable.

JENNIFER. No.

THERAPIST. So maybe you ought to acknowledge that—

JENNIFER. No!

THERAPIST. —accept what's outside your control—

JENNIFER. No, I said no.

THERAPIST. —and learn to love yourself.

JENNIFER. Love myself? What are you, a Care Bear? I can't further delay my immaculate timetable. I am a German railway conductor using a Swiss watch to operate a Japanese bullet train.

THERAPIST. You are a walking *coping mechanism*. You want an easy breakthrough? There's no such thing. A breakthrough takes mindfulness, openness, humility, sincere inquiry, and a whole lot of time.

JENNIFER. Dahhhh, why are you so bad at therapy? I can't *believe* you got four stars on Yelp.

THERAPIST. And yet *here you are*.

JENNIFER. Don't taunt me. Your bedside manner is terrible.

THERAPIST. Oh that's funny because there isn't a bed here.

JENNIFER. What do you call this? A day *bed*.

THERAPIST. I believe that's a chaise.

JENNIFER. Oh real mature. People need help here.

THERAPIST. Well then maybe "people" should have the humility to accept people's help.

JENNIFER. Yeah well this "people" is getting pretty tired of a bitch.

> *She gets a phone call.*

Hold on.

THERAPIST. Hey hey, no cell phones in here.

JENNIFER. Sorry, "This is my process." *(Answers.)* Yeah what?

ALBERT. *(Entering.)* Is therapy cutting it for ya?

JENNIFER. Oh *hell no*. I can't de-Chinese myself any more than this lady can de-stupid herself.

ALBERT. Yeah and I'd say it didn't go so well for me at the job. Insofar as I no longer have a job.

JENNIFER. Omigod Albert they FIRED YOU?!

THERAPIST. Shhh!

JENNIFER. You shhhh! You're the one who should shhhh!

ALBERT. I wanted to go Full Western but they wouldn't let me. They keep wanting to turn me into a trope. I'm sick of being the pushover Asian. But I can't be the angry Asian. But if I don't have a job I'm gonna be the old Asian lady who digs for cans in the trash.

JENNIFER. Okay Albert, I got this. If they won't let us go Full Western. Then maybe we go Full Eastern. Maybe that's the next stop on the Asian Freedom Tour!

THERAPIST. *(Derisive.) Asian Freedom Tour?*

JENNIFER. I told you to Shhhh.

ALBERT. Wait, Jen. Are you saying what I think you're saying?

JENNIFER. *Yeah.*

ALBERT. Yeaaaaahhhh.

JENNIFER. Yeaahhhhhhh.

ALBERT. Yeaahhhhhhh!!

JENNIFER. YEEAaaAAaahhHhhh!!!

ALBERT. Hell ya!

JENNIFER. Albert, we're going to China!

End of Act One

ACT TWO

Scene 1. Shenzen Special Economic Zone, China.

Jennifer and Albert enter with suitcases.

JENNIFER. This airport is *huge*.

ALBERT. It's like a whole frickin city!

JENNIFER. Albert: We're doing this.

ALBERT. Fuck ya we're doing this.

JENNIFER. Asian Freedom Tour the Motherland Edition.

ALBERT. One-way ticket. No backsies.

JENNIFER. That is… That is a thing that is happening.

ALBERT. This was a great idea, Jen.

JENNIFER. Yeah!

ALBERT. If we can't escape a racialized context in America despite being Americans, then we go be Chinese in China where race is no longer a factor.

JENNIFER. It felt kind of rash. But also quite rational. Hey, you can't spell rational without rash.

ALBERT. You can. Yo this'll be just like the Back to Africa movement!

JENNIFER. Oooh. Except I don't think that worked out. Do you think we should call Cousin Chen?

ALBERT. Whodat?

JENNIFER. Cousin Chen! I dunno. Mom said if we ever get in trouble we should call Cousin Chen.

ALBERT. You told Mom about this?

JENNIFER. Albert, I think we need guidance here. I think we should call Cousin Chen.

ALBERT. Who the fuck's Cousin Chen? No, shut up about Cousin Chen. Jen, we got this. We are going to dominate China. How are you going to dominate China?

JENNIFER. I'm gonna… I'm gonna ride a panda?

ALBERT. YAAAAAS!

JENNIFER. I'm gonna bungee jump the Great Wall!

ALBERT. Good. Good!

JENNIFER. Yo, I'm gonna try *rice* farming!

ALBERT. YESSSS.

JENNIFER. I'm gonna find an ecotourism tour that lets you do rice farming and if there's no such thing I'm gonna buy a rice hat and get into the rice patty and DO IT.

ALBERT. Question: Do you think it's a problem we don't speak Chinese?

JENNIFER. No way man. Our grandparents didn't speak English when they came to America.

ALBERT. Plus, like, I've always felt like because we're Chinese that somehow primordially we already speak it. Like even though it's one of the most complicated written and spoken languages to pick up as a second language, I feel like we'll quickly master its mouth-stretching phonemes and subtle tonalities *because* we're Chinese. That's not dumb is it?

JENNIFER. *No.* No I definitely don't think that's the stupidest thing I've ever heard in my life. Hey can I share a side thought?

ALBERT. Sure Jen what's that?

JENNIFER. I'm FREAKING OUT. I quit I quit I quit I quit my *job* over this?? I struggled *so much* to get where I am and now we're just throwing it out? It took one generation to break out of poverty, two to become middle class, and by three we're back down to immigrants? What are we gonna do, start a laundry?

ALBERT. Dude, Jen. We are not immigrants. We are *expats.*

JENNIFER. What's the difference?

ALBERT. *Immigrants* don't have a money belt stuffed with three million yuan.

> *He pats his stomach, which is hiding a hugely overstuffed money belt.*

JENNIFER. You and that money belt. Who the fuck wears a money belt?

ALBERT. Don't freak out on me Jen. There is a bright future ahead of us as soon as we step out on that curb.

> *They step forward and immediately they are swallowed by a dense throng, as personified by a cacophonous wave of unintelligible Chinese.*

Ahhh!

JENNIFER. What the?

ALBERT. Ah! What do you want?

JENNIFER. More personal space. Three foot perimeter of personal space.

ALBERT. I don't—what? Ah! What? I don't speak it.

> *Unintelligible Chinese.*

JENNIFER. English please. English or *French*.

> *Unintelligible Chinese.*

ALBERT. Ahhh! I don't know! I don't know! Just take all my money! Just take it!

> *He throws his money belt offstage and the crowd disperses.*

JENNIFER. The fuck was that?!

ALBERT. I panicked. I'm sorry.

JENNIFER. They were just *talking*.

ALBERT. Yeah but I don't speak Chinese.

JENNIFER. *Talking*. Not *robbing*.

ALBERT. You don't know that unless you speak Chinese which you don't.

JENNIFER. Was that all our money?

ALBERT. And also my passport.

JENNIFER. You moron that was both of our passports!

ALBERT. No! Why would I have *your* passport?

JENNIFER. Because, ignoramus, remember? I asked you to hold my purse while I went to the bathroom, then you said, "I'm a dude I'm not holding your purse," then I said, "You're being a goddamn

41

baby just hold my passport," then you said, "Why didn't you get a money belt like I asked," then I said, "Because what is this the '80s," then you took my passport and you put it in your stupid '80s money belt which you just threw away for no reason.

ALBERT. Well MAYBE you shouldn't have been so insistent about your dumb passport.

JENNIFER. Maybe you're an idiot.

ALBERT. Maybe you're a control freak.

JENNIFER. Maybe whenever I let you take the lead you lead us off a cliff.

ALBERT. Maybe you're so wound up you shit diamonds.

JENNIFER. Okay well *definitely* you have no leg to stand on because you just LOST OUR MONEY AND PASSPORTS.

ALBERT. That's fair.

JENNIFER. Shit man!

>*She sits.*

We have nothing now.

ALBERT. But we still have each other.

JENNIFER. Ew, no. Shut the hell up.

ALBERT. Dude, suck it up.

JENNIFER. WHAT did you say?

ALBERT. Nothing.

JENNIFER. Little boy I will END you.

ALBERT. Look I'm—

>*Cough cough.*

I'm—what do you want from me?

>*Cough.*

I said I was sorry!

JENNIFER. Get your fucking tuberculosis away from me.

>*Pause.*

Okay ya dumb ogre here's what's happening. This China nationalist rebellion is over, ya got that Chiang-Kai *Shrek*? We are marching straight to the consulate whereupon you will do whatever it takes and I do mean *whatever it takes* to get us our passports so you might wanna limber up for that because I refuse to be stuck in purgatory for the rest of my life with *you*.

ALBERT. FINE.

> *They sit apart from each other. Tzi Chuan enters.*

TZI CHUAN. Hey. *Hey.*

ALBERT. What the…?!

TZI CHUAN. So the prodigal son and daughter return.

JENNIFER. Cousin Chen?

ALBERT. Jesus?

TZI CHUAN. Neither of those.

ALBERT. Are you…are you that weird Chinese man from the park?

TZI CHUAN. Yessssss. It is I, Tzi Chuan. Did you remember my name?

ALBERT. I did not.

TZI CHUAN. The Party called me back here to acclimate you. I am a Party official, you see. And all this time you thought I was only a *crazy old man*. *Hee hee hee.*

JENNIFER. Who is this dude?

TZI CHUAN. Don't worry, we've been expecting you, Albert and Jennifer Chen.

JENNIFER. This dude knows our names?

TZI CHUAN. I know everything.

ALBERT. Off that one conversation we had in the park?

TZI CHUAN. Off of many conversations. Every time an elder Chinese sees a younger Chinese they grill them for information, and that information helps us track your whereabouts and your progress. We have a lot of friends in the community. *Mhmmmhmm-hmmm.*

ALBERT. But what do you want from us?

TZI CHUAN. We want exactly what you want. To help you fulfill your potential. But first, here's something for your ulcer. Chòu yàowù.

> *Albert takes a black sticky substance from Tzi Chuan. He*

smells it.

ALBERT. Ugggh, this smells terrible!

TZI CHUAN. *Yeaaaahhh.*

He pops it in his mouth.

JENNIFER. WHY would you eat that?!

ALBERT. *(Mouth full.)* Respect your elders.

JENNIFER. That could be *poison.*

ALBERT. Oh god I think it is poison.

JENNIFER. Spit it out.

ALBERT. No, respect! *(Swallows.)* I swallowed it *sifu.*

He does a respect-gesture thing.

TZI CHUAN. Don't worry. Chòu yàowù is just a simple compound of ginseng, ginger, burnt tea leaves.

ALBERT. Ughh, must be the *tea leaves.*

TZI CHUAN. Tiger scales. Monkey wings. Snake feet.

JENNIFER. Those…those aren't things.

ALBERT. Yo, what did I EAT?

TZI CHUAN. What matters is how you now *feel.*

ALBERT. Huh. The pain is all gone. The pain in my stomach is gone!

JENNIFER. That's just a placebo effect.

ALBERT. No, Jen, I'm cured. The ulcer is gone, and…and so is my rage. I feel my anger subsiding. I feel… I feel happy, Jen, happy!

JENNIFER. That's bullshit. Eastern medicine's bullshit.

TZI CHUAN. Chòu yàowù is a very powerful drug.

JENNIFER. Whatever creepo. We've gotta go find the consulate.

TZI CHUAN. *(Weirdly severe.)* No, Stop! *(Lightens up.)* If you please. The Party requires a *debriefing.*

JENNIFER. Listen buddy, Albert doesn't even *debrief* when he gets in the shower, so he's not gonna do it for you. Albert, let's go.

TZI CHUAN. Jennifer: We know what your struggles have been like. We know you've been misunderstood, undervalued. So for our people abroad who find life unsatisfying, there is a place for you here. There are people like you here. That's why we track you through the network of nosy Chinese.

JENNIFER. Keep talking.

TZI CHUAN. Your oncology training could be invaluable here in a country as vast as ours, industrializing at the pace that it is. You'll find that despite your preconceptions about Chinese medicine our hospitals are state of the art. I've taken the liberty of assigning you a research fellowship at a major university, along with a clinical appointment.

JENNIFER. Huuuu-what?

TZI CHUAN. That's right, stay friendly with the government and the government stays friendly with you. Think of it: No more hospital bureaucracy, litigious patients. No more begging for grants. We can lift a lot of red tape. Unless it's New Year's, in which case we'll drop a lot of red tape. *Hee hee hee*. Bureaucrat joke.

JENNIFER. You're gonna give me all that. Just like that.

TZI CHUAN. This is not like the U.S. where a foreign doctor must jump through so many hoops that they throw up their hands and go be a cabbie. We care most about the utility of worker placement— the best for the job, in the best jobs, doing their jobs best…jobs.

JENNIFER. Actually Albert's the one whose career's stalled, so…

TZI CHUAN. Yes, Albert. Your skills as a computer programmer will be highly coveted here. No longer will you be some anonymous worker contributing anonymous code to a faceless commercial conglomerate. Instead you'll be an anonymous hacker contributing anonymous government attacks on two-faced commercialist nations.

ALBERT. A hacker, no waaaaay! It's what I always wanted to do!

TZI CHUAN. But you were too scared to do it because you were obsessed with being a model minority and following all of their rules. Well in cyberspace, we *make* the rules.

ALBERT. It's like all my years of being a nerd have led up to this.

TZI CHUAN. Yes, and as for your personal lives, if you'd like we can arrange you a marriage based on our database of eligible marriage-age partners.

ALBERT. Er, that won't be necessary. I think we'll…

JENNIFER. Sign me up!

ALBERT. …Pass.

JENNIFER. Sign me the fuck up Tzi Chuan.

TZI CHUAN. I'll get you an appointment with the matchmaker. In the meantime we have a flat for you in the heart of the city. Here are the keys. Here's three million renminbi in a money belt.

ALBERT. Holy shit.

JENNIFER. Is that the same…

ALBERT. No, this money belt's made in China. The other one was made in Taiwan.

TZI CHUAN. Which means that it never existed in the first place! Ha ha haaaaa. Bureaucrat joke. Now get out there and enjoy the Shenzen Special Economic Zone! We have world-class cuisine, a bustling cityscape, a thriving underground music scene. Or if nature's your thing we have serene mountain ranges and wide rolling rivers.

ALBERT. Nope.

JENNIFER. Don't like nature.

ALBERT. Hated summer camp.

JENNIFER. I'm more of a house cat.

TZI CHUAN. Then there's also an amazing level of industry here. You can have anything custom-made to adorn your flat: bespoke furniture, bespoke fashion, bespoke spokes. For your bicycle. Sure, it may be a little smoggy, but that smog smells like *progress*. So! Do we have a deal?

JENNIFER. *(Checking in with Albert.)* I think so.

ALBERT. Sounds good to be me!

TZI CHUAN. You're ready to be Chinese nationals?

ALBERT and JENNIFER. Yeah!

TZI CHUAN. *(Sinister.)* Good. *Gooood. (Chipper.)* Then put on these breathing masks and explore modern China. *Zai jian!*

Scene 2. Chinese apartment.

Chinese apartment. It's basically the same as the Irvine place but Chinese-afied. Jennifer and Albert enter with masks on, holding boxes full of loot.

JENNIFER. I'm the Queen of the Expats!!

ALBERT. I'm Lord Expat, Duke of Expattington.

JENNIFER. I can't believe I got *three* scarves for three hundred yuan!

ALBERT. Yeah I can't believe I got three hundred dumplings for *three* yuan!

JENNIFER. Did you really have to haggle though?

ALBERT. *Yes*. It's part of their culture. I mean our culture.

JENNIFER. Should we take off our breathing masks?

> *They do. They both cough.*

ALBERT. Here pop a chòu yàowù.

JENNIFER. Oh god these smell *terrible*. UGHH.

> *They retch a little at the taste of the medicine.*

ALBERT. Wait for it…wait for it.

> *Serenity on both of their faces.*

JENNIFER and ALBERT. Ahhhh.

JENNIFER. The view from our flat is just madness!

ALBERT. I know!

JENNIFER. And the streets are so vibrant and friendly!

ALBERT. Some guy on the street's all like, "Here, buy this fish! Buy this delicious live fish mothafuckkaaaa!"

JENNIFER. How does this scarf look?

ALBERT. Ya look goooood! Want a dumpling?

JENNIFER. No thanks. Hey isn't it funny? Back home in Irvine everyone was like, "Hey, you look interesting, where are you from? No where are you *really* from?" Whereas here they're like, "Hey you *sound* interesting, where are you from?"

ALBERT. Yes yes, it's like everywhere we go we're never accepted. We're like a Discover card.

JENNIFER. Hey I have a serious question though. I love it here…

ALBERT. Me too, I so love it.

JENNIFER. But what if we're viewing China as tourists, and everything seems more exotic and vibrant than it actually is? Like in the same way others viewed us as exotic back home…

ALBERT. I didn't *get* exotic. I got *unrelatable.* Which is so unfair because the guy who sold me these dumplings was WAY more unrelatable. Didn't you find him stoic and inscrutable?

JENNIFER. There, you see? What if our very conception of China is skewed and will always be skewed, because we're coming at it as foreigners?

ALBERT. But we're not foreigners, we're authentic Chinese. And therefore our experience of China is innately authentic.

JENNIFER. I guess…

ALBERT. Yeah we've gone native now. We're living the dream! We have jobs, we own property. You have scarves.

JENNIFER. Omigod I love my scarves, it's so true.

ALBERT. God, I feel so post-racial!

JENNIFER. Suck it, America! I'm universal now. Me! I'm Beijing Beyoncé!

A knock at the door.

Who could that be?

COUSIN CHEN. *(Entering.)* At long last!

Cousin Chen gives Albert a big huge hug.

ALBERT. And you are?

Cousin Chen slaps him.

COUSIN CHEN. It's Cousin Chen! You don't recognize your own family?

JENNIFER. Oh heeeey. Cousin Chen. Right, I've heard of you.

COUSIN CHEN. Don't you see the resemblance?

JENNIFER. Totally, you look just like our mother!

She slaps Jennifer.

COUSIN CHEN. I'm from your father's side!

JENNIFER. Sorry.

COUSIN CHEN. I'm your father's sister's daughter.

JENNIFER. Right, right.

COUSIN CHEN. You never met my mother. She died before you were born. Some say of a broken heart. Others say of typhus. She missed your father *so much*. They were brother and sister separated by continents but they loved each other so dearly. Have a bag of oranges.

ALBERT. Thanks.

COUSIN CHEN. It's a very traditional gift.

JENNIFER. Is it?

COUSIN CHEN. Man you're so *whitewashed*.

JENNIFER. Cousin Chen, would you care for one of these scarves?

ALBERT. Or a dumpling? I've got like three hundred.

> *Cousin Chen laughs nervously.*

COUSIN CHEN. Why don't you turn on some music?

ALBERT. Huh? Do we even own a radio?

COUSIN CHEN. Sure you do. Turn on some music right there.

JENNIFER. O…okay.

> *She does. It's just static.*

COUSIN CHEN. Louder.

JENNIFER. What station? Or…?

COUSIN CHEN. Just louder, please.

> *Jennifer does. Cousin Chen laughs self-consciously then shuts and locks the door, checks the window, and checks the apartment.*

(Hushed tones.) Listen, you two are in danger. I would've come sooner but I was working at Foxconn and had to wait 'til the end of my sixteen-hour shift.

ALBERT. Sixteen hours?! That's terrible.

JENNIFER. I used to work eighteen hours.

ALBERT. This isn't a *contest*.

COUSIN CHEN. Please know that you're being watched. Always be on your guard. And don't fuck with the Party.

ALBERT. The Party?

COUSIN CHEN. The Party monitors everything. Don't think you're safe just because you're American.

ALBERT. Oh we're not American anymore. We're Chinese.

COUSIN CHEN. You? Yeah, no. You're about as Chinese as Mickey Rooney. So don't speak ill of the Party. Don't question Tzi Chuan. Don't eat that dumpling it has melamine in it.

She bats the dumping out of his hand.

ALBERT. No, my dumpling!

COUSIN CHEN. And these scarves contain mercury.

She snatches them.

JENNIFER. No, my scarves!

COUSIN CHEN. Wow. It's a good thing you idiots were born in America because if you were born here you'd have taken the child aptitude tests and *then* we'd see who gets to la-di-da through China and who has to do manual labor at Foxconn.

JENNIFER. Are you saying I wouldn't have passed the child aptitude tests?

COUSIN CHEN. I'm just warning you that your position is more fragile than you could possibly know.

JENNIFER. Give me the tests. I'll ace the SHIT out of a child aptitude test.

Cousin Chen slaps her.

COUSIN CHEN. This isn't the point. The point is we're family so I care about you. Please heed my warning. If you're in with the government, you can eat the best pork snout. But if you run afoul of the government, you will eat the *worst* pork snout.

JENNIFER. What if I…what if I don't want to eat any snout?

COUSIN CHEN. Don't you see? That's not an option here!

JENNIFER. You're kind of intense.

COUSIN CHEN. Stop acting like tourists! You don't look like tourists and you won't be treated that way. If you wanna stay on the Party's good side, you'd better start acting Chinese.

JENNIFER. Okay. We'll step it up.

ALBERT. We'll be better at being Chinese.

COUSIN CHEN. I have to go. My next shift starts in an hour.

JENNIFER. Cousin Chen, how can we thank you? I feel like we barely know you.

COUSIN CHEN. We're family. My mother used to cry for her lost baby brother—your father. And out of the tears from that separation comes the bond that you now share with me. Oh and don't eat the chòu yàowù—it's pure Afghan opium. Okay, love you, buh-bye.

She exits.

ALBERT. Opium. Huh.

JENNIFER.	ALBERT.
We should throw it out.	We should try some more!

ALBERT. We should throw it out, right.

Scene 3. Split scene.

Albert is at a government hacking facility, which is a militarized, Chinese-afied version of MedCo. Jennifer's at an appointment with a matchmaker, which is a Chinese-afied version of the therapist's office.

GENERAL TSO. Albert Chen?

ALBERT. Yes sir, reporting for duty.

GENERAL TSO. I've received your work clearances from Tzi Chuan. Allow me to introduce myself. I am General Tso.

Albert does a slight snicker.

What's so amusing?

ALBERT. "General Tso."

GENERAL TSO. Yes, that's my name. And Albert is your name? What

51

kind of name is that?

ALBERT. I believe it's derived from the medieval Germanic *Ad-al-ber*?

GENERAL TSO. Listen you Eurotrash, this is an elite nationalist cyberwarfare facility. You'll need a proper Chinese name.

ALBERT. But I like Albert.

GENERAL TSO. And you'll need a hacker name.

ALBERT. Oh I have a hacker name. It's Donkey-P-3-N-I-S.

GENERAL TSO. We'll find a rough translation and make that your Chinese name.

ALBERT. Deal!

GENERAL TSO. See, that's the spirit! You must wean yourself from the teat of Western degeneracy. Now. Tzi Chuan says you're good with computers?

ALBERT. The *best*.

GENERAL TSO. Ha! American modesty.

ALBERT. Sorry what I meant was the *worst*. I have much to learn from your teachings.

GENERAL TSO. Ah, then we will have no means to instruct you, for our facilities are most backwards and perhaps then you'll have to go home for we are too poor to teach you.

ALBERT. No, I mean… I do know *some* stuff about computers. I was just being humble Chinese.

GENERAL TSO. So was I. Our facilities are state of the art.

ALBERT. Oh well in that case, they're probably…too good. For one who is…unworthy…as me?

GENERAL TSO. Unworthy because you know *nothing*?

ALBERT. Well I do know *some* stuff. I actually know a fuckton of stuff.

GENERAL TSO. Again with your Western arrogance!

ALBERT. This Chinese double-speak is making my head spin.

GENERAL TSO. Then stop bragging and demonstrate your prowess through a field test.

ALBERT. Sure, what do you want me to do? Grab a credit card number? Hack into somebody's Facebook account?

GENERAL TSO. Yes, that is exactly why we created this radar-scattering bomb-resistant underground bunker. So that you could hack into Facebook, which we already block. Albert: Impress me. Showcase your skills or we have no use for you. Because this is a meritocracy here.

ALBERT. Okay General Tso. You wanna do this let's do this.

Lights shift to Jennifer and the matchmaker.

JENNIFER. Hi, there. I had an appointment with the matchmaker?

MATCHMAKER. Yes, that is my state-assigned function.

JENNIFER. Great, so let's DO THIS. Full Eastern! I stayed up all night. Here is a list of my turn-ons, here is a list of the qualities good and bad that I bring to the table, and these are my tax returns. Don't know if you need that.

MATCHMAKER. I'll take the tax returns. The rest you can keep.

She enters the data into her iPad.

JENNIFER. What about my turn-ons?

MATCHMAKER. We already have a comprehensive profile on the several signifiers that make up your pedigree: income, education, family standing, and your capacity for class mobility.

JENNIFER. Don't you consider personality factors?

MATCHMAKER. No we do not. Hold please.

JENNIFER. Excuse me, I'm trying to be more Chinese? But this road to marriage feels a *little* draconian, no?

MATCHMAKER. In America you had an online dating profile, didn't you?

JENNIFER. Well, yeah but…

MATCHMAKER. How is the government mating database any different from that?

JENNIFER. That's totally different!

MATCHMAKER. How? You select a match based on specific criteria, and so do we. It's just that we use criteria that matter.

JENNIFER. But what about what makes people "click"?

MATCHMAKER. Listen, we've been making successful matches in this country for centuries. These are lifelong matches, these are not loveless marriages. The American divorce rate is seventh in the world. Ours is fifty-seventh. So no, we do not consider what makes people "click" by including soft factors like "practices Zumba." We go by facts.

JENNIFER. Lady, you just made it onto my list of turn-ons. What does my profile say?

MATCHMAKER. Let's see. You get extremely high marks for your level of education and job standing, particularly your oncology training.

JENNIFER. Mos *Def*, son, no GAME. I'm the OG M.D./Ph.D., ask about me play*aaaaa*.

> *Pause.*

Sorry, I'm unaccustomed to praise.

MATCHMAKER. You also have extensive musical training. That shows discipline, good.

JENNIFER. *Chinese mating database*, where have you been all my life?

MATCHMAKER. Your family standing is good. You get a slight deduction for not speaking Chinese.

JENNIFER. I can learn it! Can I come back when I learn it?

MATCHMAKER. And another slight deduction for your Western-style neurosis.

JENNIFER. That's fair.

MATCHMAKER. But don't worry, we'll find someone worthy. The system's now scanning through the millions of eligible bachelors in China to find you your match.

JENNIFER. Oh hell yeah database lady! You find me Chinese Don Cheadle ya hear?

> *Lights shift.*

ALBERT. Okay General Tso. I've got you your demonstration of prowess. How about I choose an American healthcare company *at random* and eat through their servers with data worms. Let's go with—oh I don't know—MedCo Medical Software.

> *Lights up on Russ the Bus with a laptop.*

RUSS THE BUS. *(Singing.)*
> *Russ the Bus, is kill-ing minotaurs.*
> *Hack hack slash, broadsword to the face.*

What the…? Omigod omigod what is happening?? Melvin? Melvin, something is happening that I don't know what's happening. Okay okay just THINK RUSS THE BUS. You got this. Control Alt Delete! Nothing?? Omigod FUCK THIS it's every man for himself!

> *He runs across stage and offstage.*

ALBERT. So. What do we think?

GENERAL TSO. You think I don't know that was your former employer?

ALBERT. Damn.

GENERAL TSO. Oh that's right. Chinese hackers don't play.

ALBERT. Fine. You wanna see some spectacular shit? How about I hack into a series of online-enabled stereo systems and use an electrical cord exploit to short them?

> *Reggie now enters, looking admiringly offstage.*

REGGIE. Ah, just one more batch of sound systems to install and I'll have enough money to get me to Bonnaroo.

> *An electrical-short sound. Lights flicker and fog pours out from offstage.*

No! NO! I was gonna see Coldplay. COLDPLAY!!

> *Lights shift.*

ALBERT. How's that for elite hackitude, huh General Tso?

GENERAL TSO. Yes, that is a concept we can iterate on.

ALBERT. See, I know what I'm doing.

GENERAL TSO. Good. Next up, shut down the power grids in Sacramento, San Diego, and San Jose.

ALBERT. Um. Say what now.

> *Lights shift.*

> *The matchmaker's iPad dings like an Easy-Bake Oven.*

MATCHMAKER. Ah, here we are. Your perfect husband awaits.

JENNIFER. *Exciiiiting.*

MATCHMAKER. Let's see, he's a doctor…

JENNIFER. Ooh.

MATCHMAKER. Thirty-six years of age. Excellent aptitude testing. Parents are local-level Party bureaucrats and he owns property in two different cities.

JENNIFER. *Heyoooo*! Does he speak English?

MATCHMAKER. Yes, Hong Kong English. Oh, but he only works one hundred hours a week. Too bad he's so lazy.

JENNIFER. Doctors work *one hundred hours*?

MATCHMAKER. No, minimum one twenty. Is that not your standard American work week?

JENNIFER. Okay, I can handle this. Jenny just handle this. What does he look like?

MATCHMAKER. What does that matter? Don't be so shallow.

JENNIFER. Just lemme see in the profile.

MATCHMAKER. There's no photographs here.

JENNIFER. What the what? Surely you don't expect me to marry this guy sight unseen.

MATCHMAKER. Yes I do and don't call me Shirley, it's actually pronounced Shír Li.

JENNIFER. But but but what if he's a real uggo?

MATCHMAKER. Why are you being so picky, Ms. Chen? We didn't get to a billion Chinese by being so picky.

JENNIFER. But what if we don't end up happy?

MATCHMAKER. "Happy"? What's "happy"? He fits your pedigree.

JENNIFER. But don't I deserve to find *love*? Is it too much to ask to both find love and love someone worth loving?

MATCHMAKER. Yes, that is too much to ask. This is not your American rom-com.

JENNIFER. Okay. Whew. I just need a few days to think.

MATCHMAKER. Well don't think too long. I've scheduled the wedding for Friday.

JENNIFER. Wait, what? I'm not getting married this *Friday*.

MATCHMAKER. Aren't you on a timetable? Because I can assure you the rest of this country's on a very tight timetable.

JENNIFER. You know something? I'm thinking maybe what I need before getting married *next week* is to take some elaborate me time. Like maybe I should work on loving myself before loving some rando, and maybe *that's* just as valid.

MATCHMAKER. It's invalid. Ms. Chen you're betrothed. Start sewing your wedding gown.

JENNIFER. Okay, you know what? Delete my profile.

MATCHMAKER. No of course not. This is sensitive government surveillance, Ms. Chen. I mean information, not surveillance, information.

JENNIFER. Lady this is my life here. I can't believe the Chinese government's been secretly collecting all my personal data!

MATCHMAKER. Oh no, that's the U.S. government. We're very open about it.

JENNIFER. Well I'm shuttin' it down. How about I delete your whole database, huh Database Lady? How about I fuckin' do THAT? *America!*

> *She grabs the iPad.*

MATCHMAKER. Stop it, no, quit that! Ms. Chen, that's enough!

JENNIFER. Language settings! Language settings! How do you hack an iPaaaaaad?

> *Lights shift.*

GENERAL TSO. Quit stalling boy. Shut down the power grids or I'm having you court-martialed.

ALBERT. I don't… I don't know how to do it.

GENERAL TSO. Come on Albert. I know you were raised among kowtowing railwaymen but you're back in China now. Where is your national pride? Either prove your loyalty to us or go back where you came from.

ALBERT. I won't run a cyber-attack on innocent Americans.

GENERAL TSO. Aren't you disgusted with American conduct? Don't you want your revenge?

ALBERT. No in America you're s'posed to just *complain* about shit, you're not supposed to actually *do* something.

GENERAL TSO. That's really too bad because in China actions speak louder than words.

ALBERT. Too bad, foolio, I'm a maverick. I'm Clyde! Of Bonnie and Clyde!

> *He lifts a Coke can threateningly over his laptop.*

GENERAL TSO. *(Warning, as to a dog.)* NO… Don't… DO NOT…

ALBERT. Kablamo biznatch!

> *He pours the Coke on his laptop.*

GENERAL TSO. Why you seditionist American meatball!

ALBERT. *Ooot-oooh.*

> *He runs away.*
>
> *Cell-slamming sound and prison-bar gobos pop up as we transition to…*

Scene 4. Prison.

ALBERT. Going Full Eastern was a mistake.

JENNIFER. *Oh ya think?*

ALBERT. It's just—I thought there'd be room for us here. I thought we'd be Bonnie and Clyde here! But I guess we can't be Bonnie and Clyde. Cuz we're Asian.

JENNIFER. Also Bonnie and Clyde were lovers. So that's a good reason not to be Bonnie and Clyde.

ALBERT. *Whatever Jen.* What's our next move?

JENNIFER. Next move? We're locked in a Chinese jail.

ALBERT. I mean what's the next stop on our Freedom Tour?

JENNIFER. Albert I can't keep running the globe with you searching for easy fixes, I'm done.

ALBERT. So that's it then. You're saying there is no place for us.

JENNIFER. I'm saying we went on a freedom tour and landed in jail.

We *failed*, Albert. You and I? We are *losers*.

TZI CHUAN. Well well well.

ALBERT. Tzi Chuan?

TZI CHUAN. Yeah *now* you remember my name, doncha bitch.

ALBERT. Tzi Chuan, please help us!

TZI CHUAN. Oh, like you helped *me*? You made me look *foolish*.

JENNIFER. It's not fair. We're brand new to China! We never learned all the rules.

ALBERT. Tzi Chuan, please. Just give us a chance to redeem ourselves.

TZI CHUAN. I gave you that chance. Gave you everything you asked for. And you've shown yourselves to be nothing more than squabbling infants. You're an *embarrassment*. To this country, your family, your ancestors, and all forms of hominid life.

ALBERT. *Jesus.* We're sorry!

JENNIFER. Tzi Chuan, we're not fuckups okay? We may have fucked up but I have to be believe there's a well of untapped potential in us. We're highly educated! There must be some way we can still be useful to you?

TZI CHUAN. No, I see it now, see my own error. You may be educated but your minds have been poisoned by the lie of American exceptionalism. Well good job, you rugged individuals, you cacophonous deviant freaks. We're all about harmony here.

JENNIFER. We can be harmonious!

ALBERT. Yeah, we can probably—

JENNIFER. *Definitely*, we can definitely do that!

TZI CHUAN. You think yourselves capable of *harmony*?

ALBERT.	JENNIFER.
Yeeeeeaaaaaaaaahh?	Yeah! Yeah! Yeah! Yeah!

TZI CHUAN. Very well. I will release you.

ALBERT. *Oh thank God.*

TZI CHUAN. *If.* You can play me the most beautiful possible sonata.

JENNIFER. …What?

TZI CHUAN. I want you to play me something *so beautiful* it brings me to tears.

JENNIFER. Uh, like in…like in the myth of Orpheus?

TZI CHUAN. Ah?

JENNIFER. Ah?

TZI CHUAN. Ah?

JENNIFER. Ah?

TZI CHUAN. Ah?

JENNIFER. Don't "ah-ah" me. You know: the Greek myth of Orpheus.

TZI CHUAN. *(As though he understands.)* Ah ah ah! I don't give a *shit* about your Greek myth. At any rate, if you can play me the most beautiful possible *tear-inducing* sonata, you may go free.

JENNIFER. You don't happen to have a piano in here, or…?

TZI CHUAN. Yes, over there.

JENNIFER. Oh! How'd I miss that?

TZI CHUAN. "Is there a piano?" It's Chinese prison, not Chinese hell… And for you. Albert. You may choose between this beaten-up Western cello or this erhu, the traditional Chinese two-stringed violin with a resonator box covered in python skin. Choose wisely.

JENNIFER. Albert, this is it. This is what all those years and years of musical training have been for!

ALBERT. Shit man. I haven't played the cello in years.

JENNIFER. Then pick up that erhu and let's fiddle our way to freedom.

ALBERT. What, the erhu? No, I gotta go for the cello. I'm a former concert cellist.

JENNIFER. No this is some kind of *Indiana Jones* Holy Grail test. You gotta go erhu.

ALBERT. *You* go erhu.

JENNIFER. I'm a concert fucking *pianist* Albert. I'm not going erhu, you go erhu.

ALBERT. It's made of *python skin.*

JENNIFER. So the fuck what?

ALBERT. *(To Tzi Chuan.)* I'll take the cello.

JENNIFER. Daaawwww.

TZI CHUAN. Very well. Play for your freedom.

> *Albert picks up the cello. The two play the most beautiful possible sonata. Maybe a cut from the Schubert Arpeggione Sonata. It's moving and genuine, and for once the two of them move together as a unit seamlessly. This is perhaps the most soulful thing we've seen from these two wretches all evening. We enter a flashback in voiceovers.*

MOM. Jennifer look: a *piano*. Do you think you might want to try it?

> *Time passes.*

Albert look how your sister's playing *piano*. You think maybe *you'd* like to learn to play cello?

ALBERT. No.

DAD. Well too bad you're doing it anyway.

> *Time passes.*

MOM. Kids! If you want to earn first chair in school orchestra you have to sound perfect.

JENNIFER. Okay Mom, we'll practice twice as hard.

ALBERT. I don't wanna do this! I'm no good at cello.

DAD. How would you know? You're seven. I promise you nothing worth doing comes without struggle.

> *Time passes.*

JENNIFER. I can play Beethoven!

ALBERT. I *am* Beethoven!

JENNIFER. Fine, then I'm Gustav Mahler.

ALBERT. No I wanna be Mahler!

JENNIFER. No one wants to be Mahler you just wanna copycat me.

> *Time passes.*

MOM. Kids, if you want to get into national youth orchestra you have to sound perfect.

ALBERT. We practice four hours a day!

MOM. No more birthday parties. No more skateboarding. And no more talking on the phone all night Jenny.

JENNIFER. I should be playing a solo. Why do I have to be saddled with him?

ALBERT. So play on your own I don't need you.

DAD. You two will play the duet and that's final.

MOM. Trust us, you're much better off as a unit.

> *Time passes.*

JENNIFER. Can you come in more *affettuoso* right there?

ALBERT. *Affettuoso* or *amoroso*. How about *misterioso*!

JENNIFER. I think you are o-so lame-o.

> *Time passes.*

Let's go again.

> *Time passes.*

Let's go again.

> *Time passes.*

Go again.

ALBERT. I can't anymore.

JENNIFER. One more time, please? For me?

> *Time passes.*

ALBERT. You're still here??

JENNIFER. This one part keeps getting me. It has to be perfect.

ALBERT. You do know it's your birthday today?

JENNIFER. So sit. Play it with me.

> *Time passes.*

ALBERT. Jen once you go to college. You think that we'll keep doing this?

JENNIFER. What, playing music? Of course we will. You and me? We're a team.

> *Time passes.*

MOM. Kids! If you want to make it to Carnegie Hall—

DAD. Wait honey, listen.

MOM. It's perfect. I don't believe it. It's perfect.

DAD. Shhh. Let them play.

> *They finish the flashback, the duet. Tzi Chuan cries silently.*

62

ALBERT. You're crying.

TZI CHUAN. Yes… Because that was TERRIBLE.

ALBERT. WHAT?

TZI CHUAN. *TURRIBLE*. You practiced music all your life to play *this*? You are garbage.

JENNIFER. You take that back. Our sonata was awesome!

ALBERT. It's my fault. I'm rusty.

JENNIFER. No, it's my fault, I rushed the first phrase.

TZI CHUAN. No, it's both of your faults. My ears are attuned to the pentatonic scale, not that Western heptatonic horseshit. You shoulda gone erhu.

JENNIFER. God*dammit* Albert.

TZI CHUAN. For your crimes you are hereby sentenced to re-education.

JENNIFER. That doesn't sound bad. I love education!

TZI CHUAN. Ah-ah, I said *re*-education.

JENNIFER. What's the dif?

TZI CHUAN. Education is the centerpiece of our Eastern values, whereas *re*-education is a euphemism for grueling physical exertion in a remote outdoor camp.

JENNIFER. Physical education?!

ALBERT. Summer camp?!

JENNIFER and ALBERT. NOOOOO!

TZI CHUAN. Fare thee well shitheads.

He exits. A moment of stillness.

JENNIFER. You played *really beautifully*.

ALBERT. I know. So did you.

JENNIFER. We haven't played together in *years*. Albert *we did that*.

ALBERT. So what if we did? We're still here.

JENNIFER. Yeah but all those years playing music and we never stopped to appreciate it. Or each other.

ALBERT. I guess that wasn't on Mom and Dad's *checklist*.

JENNIFER. I'm saying look what we're capable of. Our parents didn't fail us, Albert, look at these gifts we've been given.

ALBERT. *Some gifts.*

JENNIFER. Albert I think we oughta be more grateful to our family.

ALBERT. Grateful for what, exactly? We are in PRISON Jen. It's not like our family can save us from that.

> *Tzi Chuan screams from offstage.*

What was *that*?

COUSIN CHEN. *(Enters, bloody.)* Hey...hey...

ALBERT. Cousin Chen? What the hell happened to you?

COUSIN CHEN. Don't worry it's mostly Tzi Chuan's blood. Nope... nope a lot of that's my blood.

JENNIFER. How'd you get in here?

COUSIN CHEN. I stabbed Tzi Chuan's heart out, that's how. Here, take these passports. They're fakes. You can't use your real names anymore. Take the passports...here, take them.

ALBERT. Cousin Chen, you did this, for us?

JENNIFER. But we barely know you.

COUSIN CHEN. Family is everything, no?

ALBERT. But...

COUSIN CHEN. Don't worry. I was made to suffer. We were all made to suffer. The Chinese capacity for endurance creates great things—the Great Wall, the Forbidden City, the opening to the Beijing Olympics. So cold...

JENNIFER. Cousin Chen. Cousin Chen, no, stay with us.

COUSIN CHEN. I regret...not finishing...

> *She dies. She reanimates.*

Not finishing!

> *She dies. She reanimates.*

Not finishing the aluminum casing on those last twenty iPads! Okay, love you, buh-bye.

> *She dies for real.*

JENNIFER. Holy shit.

Scene 5. Customs.

Airplane sound. Jennifer and Albert enter. A customs guy is waiting.

VOICEOVER 1. Welcome to LAX. Please proceed to immigration. The estimated wait time is…

VOICEOVER 2. Sixty

VOICEOVER 1. Hours.

CUSTOMS GUY. Next? Passports, visas, and paperwork.

    They step forward.

Step back please.

    They do.

Give me your passports!

    They step forward.

Step back I said!

    They do.

And you are… Xiao Xīnzàng and Xiao Xīnyuàn.

JENNIFER. Yep.

CUSTOMS GUY. Did I say that right?

JENNIFER. Sure, okay.

CUSTOMS GUY. *(To Albert.)* Hey buddy. I'm not sure I'm liking your tone.

ALBERT. I didn't… I didn't *say anything*.

JENNIFER. Be cool okay?

ALBERT. *You be cool.*

CUSTOMS GUY. Is there a problem here, Xiao Xīnzàng?

ALBERT and JENNIFER. No problem Officer sorry.

CUSTOMS GUY. Excuse me, I was talking to Xiao Xīnzàng.

ALBERT and JENNIFER. My mistake.

    Pause.

You go ahead.

> *Pause.*

No you go.

JENNIFER. Shit.

CUSTOMS GUY. Wait, which one of you is Xiao Xīnzàng and which one is Xiao Xīnyuàn?

ALBERT. Okay, here's the deal. Our real names are—

JENNIFER. Both.

> *Pause.*

We don't know which is which. Our parents left us at an orphanage after being mauled by Manchurian snow leopards.

CUSTOMS GUY. Those fucking snow leopards. So tragic, so many orphans.

ALBERT. *(To Jen.)* Dude what are you DOING?

CUSTOMS GUY. Okay, yeah. Now I'm *really* not liking your tone.

JENNIFER. I'm sorry, Officer, he's in mourning. We both are. Our cousin just died and…

CUSTOMS GUY. What died? Died of what? Bird flu? Swine flu? SARS? Swine flu ebola SARS? Have you been in contact with any sick pigs? Because Customs Form Item 6A clearly states: Mark X if you've had sexual congress with any livestock, poultry, or pigs.

ALBERT. Sir, you dishonor me and my family.

CUSTOMS GUY. I'm doing my job.

ALBERT. You're doing your job with particular relish, imposing a higher bar of entry upon us because you lack empathy.

JENNIFER. Ha ha ha, old Chinese proverb! As I was saying my brother *Xiao* over here is feeling emotional over our cousin. Who was stabbed to death. All very normal.

CUSTOMS GUY. Stabbed to death. Was it ninjas or Triads?

JENNIFER. I'm gonna sayyyyy Triads?

ALBERT. Yo: I disagree with your *choices.*

JENNIFER. *Shutttttt upppppppppp.*

CUSTOMS GUY. Moving on then. According to these documents your occupation is… Peasant?

JENNIFER. *(Twinges.)* …Correct.

CUSTOMS GUY. Okay and highest level of education attained is…junior academy for C-level peasants.

JENNIFER. *(She's like practically going to cry.)* …Correct.

CUSTOMS GUY. And your place of residence is… Shenzen Peasant Sector Special Development Zone for Ignorant Peasants.

JENNIFER. *(Like seriously crying.)* Uh-huh…

CUSTOMS GUY. You speak really good by the way. Really Good English. *(Asian accent.) Sank you very muuuush.*

ALBERT. Okay, *no.* You know something? Fuck this. I'm not Xiao-whatever. *She's* not Xiao-whatever. And we're not fucking peasants, we both went to goddam *Harvard.*

JENNIFER. *Xiao,* cut it out.

CUSTOMS GUY. You do know that none of what you're saying matches these documents?

JENNIFER. *(Whispered.)* What are you doing?

ALBERT. *(Whispered.)* This guy is a prick.

JENNIFER. *(Whispered.)* So the fuck what suck it up. Cousin Chen sacrificed *everything* getting us here.

ALBERT. *(Whispered.)* If we're not seen as equals what good is our freedom? Is bigotry not also a prison?

JENNIFER. *(Whispered.)* HEY I am not gonna debate racial injustice with you in the middle of *LAX frickin' airport.* I just frickin wanna go *home.*

CUSTOMS GUY. Oh you're going home all right. On the next flight to China.

JENNIFER. Oh. You can hear us whispering.

CUSTOMS GUY. *Yeah.*

ALBERT. Look our real names are Albert and Jennifer Chen. We were both born in Irvine.

CUSTOMS GUY. You do know that passport fraud is a serious crime.

ALBERT. Whoa whoa whoa, nobody's committing a fraud here. We just assumed different names for the purpose of willfully deceiving the government.

CUSTOMS GUY. But that's…that's the definition of fraud.

ALBERT. We had to do it to get out of China.

CUSTOMS GUY. Oh so you're dissidents? I've heard of that. You're, like, Chinese political dissidents seeking asylum.

ALBERT. No, we're citizens.

CUSTOMS GUY. Chinese citizens.

ALBERT. *American* citizens.

CUSTOMS GUY. Naturalized out of China.

ALBERT. No, we're not naturalized, we were born here, you jackass!

CUSTOMS GUY. I beg your pardon.

ALBERT. Naw, man, that's racist.

CUSTOMS GUY. Oh, I'm sorry, you arrive on a plane from China, your passports and visas say you're Chinese, the Chinese government says you're Chinese, but when I say you're Chinese I'm a racist.

ALBERT. Don't try to logic me, racist!

JENNIFER. Look, our parents live in San Marino—just call them and ask!

CUSTOMS GUY. Oh okay, let me just pick up my finger phone.

He mimes a phone.

Oh nope, they're not answering because my finger phone's fake and so is your story.

ALBERT. You're not *listening* to us!

CUSTOMS GUY. That's because your thick Chinese accents preclude me from engaging with you on a human level.

JENNIFER. What accents? Do we sound foreign to you?

CUSTOMS GUY. I don't hear race.

ALBERT. But isn't our heritage infinitely fascinating? Don't you want to know where we're *really* from?

JENNIFER. I know you'd like our history to fall into easy narratives but the truth is more complicated, and you're just going to have to accept that and hear our full story.

CUSTOMS GUY. Who am I, Ira Glass? I don't have time for that. My job is to make quick judgments about who's American and who's not, so if you want to be in this country I suggest you make your story as easy on me as possible. Now these passports look legit but your story sounds balls-out wacko, so what's it gonna be? Either enter the U.S. as the foreign Chinese peasants you appear to be, or persist in this thin claim to American citizenship but you will be detained here indefinitely until the judge hears your cocked-up fabulation at which point you'll go back where you came from. Up to you.

ALBERT. … …Fine. I'll be Xiao-something. She'll be Xiao-something too.

CUSTOMS GUY. Cool beans. Welcome to America.

He stamps the passports.

Frickin lunatics.

Customs guy exits.

JENNIFER. Look, I know what you're thinking. At least we live to fight another day?

ALBERT. Not if we never fought to begin with. If we do nothing to challenge his preconceptions, nothing ever changes and no one's the better for it.

JENNIFER. I know, but if you keep going balls out over every fucked-up encounter, your stomach will burn through and you'll *die* and then who wins?

ALBERT. Jen is this progress to you? Three generations in and we're back down to immigrants. Three generations in and we don't even have our real names. Are you really willing to settle for being no better off than our grandparents?

JENNIFER. *No.* But at the same time we have to be grateful for the countless sacrifices our family made getting us here. I mean, for their sake what else can we do but endure?

Mom and Dad enter.

MOM. Finally some sense out of you.

ALBERT. Mom? Dad?

JENNIFER. You're here?

DAD. Of course we're here.

ALBERT. If you're here then why didn't you help us?

DAD. You know why. We had to trust you to figure things out on your own.

JENNIFER. How'd you even know we were here?

MOM. We have a lot of friends in the community dear.

ALBERT. Wait, the *airport* community? How did you really know?

MOM. We had dog microchips installed in you when you were babies.

ALBERT. Dude. What??

DAD. Yes, if you love someone, set them free—with a dog microchip.

ALBERT. WHAT??

JENNIFER. Frankly I'm surprised you're surprised by this. *(To parents.)* Hey. So. I'm sorry our last visit got out of hand.

DAD. You're figuring out your place in the world. We had to do it.

MOM. So how was your *trip*? I assume you solved racism.

ALBERT. No because it takes *work* to solve racism and none of you are willing to do that work. We're being suppressed, our humanity's being taken from us, and it never changes, not in China and for damn sure not here. I know you want to ignore it. Well I can't.

DAD. We never *ignored* it. We fought damn hard. Albert, I think you're undervaluing your family's successes here.

ALBERT. But we don't define success like you do. Our jobs and our grades and degrees.

DAD. Even so, the fact that your family has thrived here? *Is* the change that you seek. Our family's very presence here defies pre-conception.

MOM. Which is why we pushed you so hard. The longer we're here and the higher we reach, the more they're gonna have to deal with the fact we're not going away.

DAD. It's your turn now.

ALBERT. My *turn*. To keep this family afloat while being weighed down by pervasive systemic racism.

DAD. Yep. Don't fuck it up for me boy.

ALBERT. But. But if glacial generational progress is the solution that's like lifetimes away. I'm choking on my own blood. Jen, don't you feel like we're homeless?

JENNIFER. Albert I got you. If you know that at least your family gets you, can that be enough for today?

ALBERT. And tomorrow?

MOM. *(Defiant.)* Oh tomorrow we'll still be here.

DAD. Chens don't quit.

JENNIFER. That's right, because regardless of what anyone else thinks? Look around you Albert. We *are* home. This. Is our home.

> *He looks around and exhales.*

End of Play

PROPERTY LIST

(Use this space to create props lists for your production.)

SOUND EFFECTS

(Use this space to create sound effects lists for your production.)

Dear reader,

Thank you for supporting playwrights by purchasing this acting edition! You may not know that Dramatists Play Service was founded, in 1936, by the Dramatists Guild and a number of prominent play agents to protect the rights and interests of play-wrights. To this day, we are still a small company committed to our partnership with the Guild, and by proxy all playwrights, established and aspiring, working in the English language.

Because of our status as a small, independent publisher, we respect-fully reiterate that this text may not be distributed or copied in any way, or uploaded to any file-sharing sites, including ones you might think are private. Photocopying or electronically distributing books means both DPS and the playwright are not paid for the work, and that ultimately hurts playwrights everywhere, as our profits are shared with the Guild.

We also hope you want to perform this play! Plays are wonderful to read, but even better when seen. If you are interested in performing or producing the play, please be aware that performance rights must be obtained through Dramatists Play Service. This is true for *any* public performance, even if no one is getting paid or admission is not being charged. Again, playwrights often make their sole living from performance royalties, so performing plays without paying the royalty is ultimately a loss for a real writer.

This acting edition is the **only approved text for performance**. There may be other editions of the play available for sale from other publishers, but DPS has worked closely with the playwright to ensure this published text reflects their desired text of all future productions. If you have purchased a revised edition (sometimes referred to as other types of editions, like "Broadway Edition," or "[Year] Edition"), that is the only edition you may use for perfor-mance, unless explicitly stated in writing by Dramatists Play Service.

Finally, this script cannot be changed without written permission from Dramatists Play Service. If a production intends to change the script in any way—including casting against the writer's intentions for characters, removing or changing "bad" words, or making other cuts however small—without permission, they are breaking the law. And, perhaps more importantly, changing an artist's work. Please don't do that!

We are thrilled that this play has made it into your hands. We hope you love it as much as we do, and thank you for helping us keep the American theater alive and vital.

Note on Songs/Recordings, Images, or Other Production Design Elements

Be advised that Dramatists Play Service, Inc., neither holds the rights to nor grants permission to use any songs, recordings, images, or other design elements mentioned in the play. It is the responsibility of the producing theater/organization to obtain permission of the copyright owner(s.) for any such use. Additional royalty fees may apply for the right to use copyrighted materials.

For any songs/recordings, images, or other design elements mentioned in the play, works in the public domain may be substituted. It is the producing theater/organization's responsibility to ensure the substituted work is indeed in the public domain. Dramatists Play Service, Inc., cannot advise as to whether or not a song/arrangement/recording, image, or other design element is in the public domain.